UNDISPUTED

UNDIS

DONOVAN BAILEY

PUTED

A CHAMPION'S LIFE

RANDOM HOUSE CANADA

PUBLISHED BY RANDOM HOUSE CANADA

www.penguinrandomhouse.ca

Random House Canada and colophon are registered trademarks.

Library and Archives Canada Cataloguing in Publication

Title: Undisputed : a champion's life / Donovan Bailey.
Names: Bailey, Donovan, 1967- author.
Description: Includes index.
Identifiers: Canadiana (print) 20230182968 | Canadiana (ebook) 20230182984 | ISBN 9781039005143 (hardcover) | ISBN 9781039005150 (EPUB)
Subjects: LCSH: Bailey, Donovan, 1967- | LCSH: Sprinters—Canada—Biography. | LCSH: Athletes, Black—Canada—Biography. | CSH: Jamaican Canadians—Biography. | LCGFT: Autobiographies.
Classification: LCC GV1061.15.B45 A3 2023 | DDC 796.42/2092—dc23

Text design: Matthew Flute
Jacket design: Matthew Flute
Image credits: Gilbert Iundt / Contributor / Getty Images

Printed in Canada

10 9 8 7 6 5 4 3 2 1

Penguin
Random House
KNOPF CANADA

For George and Daisy,
Adrienna, Mateus, Maximus and Marcus,
With love, undisputed.

CONTENTS

PROLOGUE

I DIDN'T PLAN TO SAY IT. I hadn't thought it through. But in the heat of the moment, after I destroyed a television, I blurted it out:

"When I'm the king here and I run shit, this will never happen!"

That moment changed my life. I had put my business career on hold, and now I was at a crossroads in my track career, too.

Let me explain.

It's 1993 and I was with the Canadian national team in Stuttgart, Germany, ahead of the World Championships. I was one of the top sprinters in the country at this point and travelled to Europe with the intention of competing in the 100- and 200-metre events, along with the men's 4x100-metre relay. That didn't happen.

I was at the track with my fellow sprinters—Glenroy Gilbert, Bruny Surin, Atlee Mahorn, among others—winding my body down after practice, a few days before the relay competition, when Mike Murray, a coach with Team Canada, approached me. He delivered his message quickly—that I wasn't going to be competing in any individual competitions at Stuttgart, and that I should prepare for the relay—then walked away. It felt like a sucker-punch.

Here I was thinking my star had risen in track and field. I was hitting my stride as a sprinter. I could taste success. However, Canadian officials thought otherwise, and I felt in my heart I had been slighted. Only one of the sprinters selected ahead of me had beaten me in head-to-head competition, and my times were rapidly improving. His were not. There was no limit in sight to my abilities in the 100-metre, and I was cutting through the ranks of my own team at a pace no coach or competitor could deny. But they denied it anyway, and I was relegated in Stuttgart to just the relay team.

My mind was racing, but quitting was not an option. I had to double down on my sprinting career and push even harder. The worst thing anybody can say to me is that I can't do something. And I sure as hell wasn't going to sit back and allow myself to be moved around someone's strategy board like a piece of property, which was how the Canadian athletes were too often treated. I'd watched Carl Lewis, the great American track athlete, who always got paid like the star attraction he was. I'd watched the ascendance of Michael Jordan, who could be coached only by the very best in basketball. I'd watched Muhammad Ali. I'd watched Tiger Woods. Many people couldn't handle a Black athlete who didn't accept his place. And I was surrounded by too many people who thought they could tell me mine. Too many people who had once told another Canadian sprinter, Ben Johnson, his place. You probably know how that turned out. If not, we'll get to it.

No chance were any of these people going to run my career. When I came across Murray outside our residence in the athletes' village later that afternoon, I saw red.

I reamed him out and said some things I probably shouldn't repeat. Then I stormed inside. Glenroy Gilbert, my teammate and close friend, was trying to talk me down. He understood my disappointment—us 100-metre guys were typically wound up pretty tight—but there was more going on in my head that I hadn't yet found the words to express. After venting to him, I reached for the television that was sitting on a nearby table, ripped the plug from the outlet and threw the TV across the room. I stared at the massive hole in the drywall for a moment, and that's when the words came to me.

"When I'm the king here and I run shit, this will never happen!"

※

There's a story told by Tiger Woods, shared during his World Golf Hall of Fame induction speech in 2022, that stands out for me: "Playing at some of these golf courses, I was not allowed in the clubhouses where all the other juniors were. The colour of my skin dictated that. As I got older, that drove me even more. So, as I was denied access into the clubhouses, that's fine. Put my shoes on here in the parking lot. I asked two questions only, that was it: Where was the first tee, and what was the course record."

That, to me, is how a champion speaks. Winners either find their way or they make one. For the champion, ceilings are imaginary. People all decide whether we want to accept or ignore the limitations that ceilings are meant to impose. Champions accept no ceilings. Woods, Lewis, Ali, Jordan—and me.

Back to Stuttgart. Sure, I wasn't the king of anything yet, or a champion—and I didn't run shit. I didn't even run in the relay that week. But my statement was a promise to myself. I was going to find my own path and achieve such a high level of success that no coach or ruling body would tell me what I could and could not do. Nobody would tell me to know my place and leave the decisions to the officials. Especially these officials, some of them the very people who had been in charge five years earlier, when Canada's track and field team had embarrassed the sport and disgraced the country.

I came into track and field from outside their little world. They were used to dealing with athletes from a different socio-economic class. Urban kids who didn't have clear routes to prosperity, some the children of new Canadians who'd come to the country with very little. Some of the athletes had come to Canada themselves as children, and a contract with Athletics Canada was a chance to elevate themselves and their families from difficult circumstances. That wasn't me.

Yes, I'd moved to Canada as a kid, but I'd given up a job on Bay Street in my twenties to pursue my athletic career. And I could go back to Canada's financial centre at a moment's notice. My dad had taught me many things, like how to make money and be no one's fool. So unlike the athletes these coaches and administrators were used to pushing around, I knew how things worked in the real world. I knew how to build a business and manage myself like a brand.

I was going to take charge of Donovan Bailey, Inc., and make myself the dominant brand in track and field—the greatest athlete my country, maybe the world, had ever seen.

That's exactly what I did.

I let people run with their narratives of me, too. Say what they want. That's the way I collect data on people I deal with and decide what I want to do. Since I was a kid, I've listened closely and asked a lot of questions. That's how I learned then, and that's how I learned things about Canada's athletic establishment that it doesn't seem to know about itself. I promised myself one day I'd take my story back, tell it in my own way.

And that's exactly what I've done.

CHAPTER 1

THE WHY KID

EVERYONE'S CHILDHOOD has a moment that stands out. It could be a traumatic event or a small, joyous encounter. Either way, these moments stick in our heads for one reason or another and inform the person that we become. One of those moments came for me when I was twelve years old.

I was sitting beside my mom on a bus. When I looked out the window, I could see my birth country in its full splendour. Man, Jamaica is a beautiful place. We were driving by the coast just then, so I was entranced by ocean waves lapping against the shore. A little farther along, we were inland and cows were grazing on green fields. As we drove out of the countryside, we entered the hustle and bustle of the city, and I could hear it all from the back seat—horns honking, loud conversations in patois, reggae blaring from stereo speakers.

The chaos outside was juxtaposed to the tranquility on the bus. There was reggae playing on the radio, "Nice Up the Dance" by Papa Michigan & General Smiley. Just thinking of that song makes me happy. I don't know if there was ever a song on the radio during my entire childhood that made me upset. I attribute that to my mom. She ensured that my brothers and I were always in a good mood. She had a knack for always putting us at ease and making us feel comfortable.

One of the things my mom used to do, especially when she could sense I was becoming pensive, was start talking to me in a soft tone while giving me a scalp massage. It always calmed me down, sometimes even put me to sleep, and she continued to do it throughout her life. If she were alive today, I know we would still have conversations like that, with me reclining and her hands on top of my head as if I were still a little boy in need of his mother's calming influence. I trusted my mother more than anyone.

During this moment in the bus, though, I noticed something was different. I looked up at my mom and realized that although she was as calm as ever, she was not her usual serene self. She had tears in her eyes. I knew why. And I knew that her tears were a mix of immense joy and deep sadness. I was just a boy at the time, but even then, certain truths had become apparent. One was that this woman loved me more than she loved life itself. Secondly, I knew that whatever I did in my life and wherever I went, I would be representing this person. So, I needed to be damn sure that whatever I did, I was honouring and respecting her.

✳

I was born on December 16, 1967, in Manchester, Jamaica. We lived surrounded by farms and fields, deep in the green mountains of the island's interior. Everywhere around us, the brightly painted houses of our friends and neighbours burst in little pops of colour from between the trees. The mountain breeze stirred the canopy, carrying a hint of salt from the ocean, so far away we couldn't see it from our home. It wasn't how most people picture Jamaica, if they've only ever been to its beaches, but make no mistake it was paradise.

Who were *we*? I have four brothers—Glenroy is the oldest (not to be confused with Glenroy my fellow sprinter), followed by Wilburn, O'Neil, myself and the youngest boy, Michael. My father was named George and my mother Daisy.

In my opinion, my mother was the most stunningly beautiful woman in the world. Standing at five foot one, she was dark-skinned with straight-ish hair, and she always exuded a peaceful energy. She was the backbone of her household and a firecracker who never yelled but always got her way. She taught me how to communicate. Any oration skills I possess, along with the ability to be convincing without raising my voice, came from her. If you haven't guessed by now, I'm an unapologetic mama's boy. I don't care if anyone has anything to say about that; it's just how I am.

My dad was, well, let's start by saying he was a very Jamaican man. He was a hard worker and didn't communicate *with* us.

Instead, he communicated *to* us. Unlike most parents now, including me, who speak to their children directly and have dialogues with them, my dad would tell me what to do—right down to how I would spend my Saturday morning once my homework was done. There was no dialogue, no discussion.

When I was four years old, my mom wanted me to take piano lessons. We went to the teacher's house, and as I sat down on the bench in front of the ivory keys, I heard the sounds of children my age cheering and shouting. I peeped out the window and saw them playing football (with the British influence in Jamaica, we didn't call it "soccer"). Even the son of the piano instructor was out there on the grass, enjoying himself. I hated being stuck indoors and wanted to join them so badly. I knew, even at that age, that if I were to have any chance of getting away from the piano bench, it wasn't going to be through my dad. I could always express myself to my mother, so I told her, "Mom, I don't want to do this." However, being heard and being let off the hook are two different things. My dad soon learned of my request, and he responded with a lesson I've never forgotten, saying, "No, son. We love you, but you signed up for it, so you're going to finish. You're going to go through and understand that when you sign up for something, you make a commitment to it. You're going to finish it." Even at that very young age, that way of thinking was instilled in me. It seemed strict at the time, but the reality is that I grew up with parents who were incredibly supportive. They showed confidence in me. It gave me structure, and I'm grateful for it.

That structure was emphasized every Sunday morning. There were three aspects of life for us: school, church and sports. In that order. So, even if it wasn't a school day, Sunday was not for sleeping in. We were a Christian family and attended Mount Olivet United Church. During the years that I was part of youth fellowship, I would wake up at 7:00 a.m., walk to church and stay for the 11:00 a.m. service. That was just a fact—nobody was waking me and telling me to get moving and get dressed. Self-motivation was instilled in me by my family and surroundings from my earliest days and became inherent. People at the church noticed my leadership abilities and recruited me at age nine to become a junior Sunday school teacher, which added to my parents' efforts to make me an emotionally mature youngster.

When I reflect on my childhood, I'm proud of the fact that I grew up without my parents or anyone else patting me on the shoulder for every effort or trying to push me to complete whatever task was before me. My parents' messaging to my brothers and me was a little simpler: *This is what you do and this is when you're going to do it*. And you got it done, no questions asked. I can remember when, at age four, I got the opportunity to share a bunk bed with my older brother O'Neil. I had to take the bottom bunk because I was younger, but my mom made sure even then that as soon as my eyes opened, I was to start the day properly—there would be no special rules for the little brother. That entailed making my bed, brushing my teeth and washing my face. Even as a preschooler, I had to be independent and responsible. That discipline would serve me through life.

As a kid who loved being outdoors, I grew up in the right place: out in the country. Manchester is a parish located in the central part of Jamaica, about ninety kilometres from the capital,

Kingston. We lived on a farm that had been passed down through generations of my mother's family. From the mountainside on which it was situated, you could look out over acres and acres of beautiful, lush, green forest and grass. We were so far inland we couldn't see the ocean, even from up so high. I think the wonder of that imagery has been seared into my DNA. It's the reason that even today, my greatest peace comes when I am surrounded by trees and land. As a child, I could get lost as if in a dream, gazing off into the distance.

On the farm, we grew our own ground provisions and never went hungry. We had carrots, lettuce, yams, plantain and cassava, all of which was put to use by my mother, who was a wonderful cook. In her kitchen, which was in an outbuilding just behind the house, she prepared oxtail, curried goat and many other delectable specialties. We raised every animal that you could conceivably raise in Jamaica—goats, pigs, chickens, you name it. We enjoyed fresh milk from the cows every morning. Sometimes when people learn how I grew up, they ask if I had any favourite animals back on that farm. The question makes me smile. I mean, in Jamaica, we love animals, and they sometimes grazed right up near the house, but at the end of the day an animal is livestock. As a kid, I developed an understanding that at some point this animal could be dinner. We had lots of dogs, too, and there was a special pup named Rex. He was mine. But even so, back home, a dog had its place—and that was outside. When I eventually moved to Canada, I could not understand the concept of having a dog inside the house, the kitchen and even the bed. In the West Indies, we just viewed canines differently. They were there to guard the property.

My brothers and I didn't spend much time tending to the animals. We helped when help was needed. Of course, we had household chores—making our beds, washing dishes, helping our mother cook—but the farm was mostly handled by people we hired and extended family. For my brothers and me, our mom and dad made academics our priority. My father was never in the stands watching his sons play school sports. Not one time. However, he was *always* at the parent-teacher meetings. And he'd arrive an hour early, ready to discuss how his children were faring in their academic lives.

There is a misconception that exists about Jamaica and the rest of the Caribbean. People often think that sports and music are our main priorities and career aspirations. That's simply wrong. Every single parent in the West Indies places an inordinate emphasis on education. I've had Asian friends over the course of my life whose parents hailed from China or India, and they've told me that the expectation from their families was that they become a doctor, lawyer or engineer. Everything else was perceived as "lesser than." We were raised with a similar mindset in Jamaica. Maybe it wasn't that specific in terms of profession, but the gist was the same—education represented the best route to success.

I used to walk to Mount Olivet Primary School each day. There were no buses, and so, arriving on time was the responsibility of the student, even at that tender age. Because of Jamaica's history as a British colony, our education system was not too different from what a child in the UK would experience. I'll never forget the disciplinary elements built into the school, in part because I feel that it helped shape me as a person. When we arrived at school, teachers would run a comb through our hair to make sure it was neat and clean. They would also check for sweat. Yes, you read that correctly. If a child was sweating, that meant they had left home too late and needed to run to school. Can you imagine that happening to a student in Canada? There would be protests. But that was life back in Jamaica in the 1970s. And, of course, I was reprimanded for sweating. There were times I'd be messing around before school with my younger brother, Michael, and suddenly realize that I was late. So, I would sprint to school and try to dry myself before I reached the front door. It wouldn't work. I'd get a couple slaps and go to class. That was it.

If I'm honest, I was lazy as a student. Success came easy at school, so it impacted my effort. I routinely finished my class-work early, and some teachers would give me extra work so I didn't disturb the other students. "Donovan, you're done? Take some extra. Here's an opportunity to do a little more. Here's an opportunity to read some more." I would do it, though I didn't try that hard. I guess you could say I needed to be constantly stimulated. I have a photographic memory and could study for literally an hour, write the test and achieve whatever marks I needed in that exam. My father knew that, and by the time I was eight years old, he used to remark that I should be a lawyer.

Not only was I a quick study, he called me the "why kid" because of my inquisitive nature. Every time I'd have a conversation with an adult, I'd pepper them with an endless stream of questions: "But why?" "Why did that man become president?" "Why is Muhammad Ali the greatest fighter in the world?" "Tell me more." I wasn't trying to start an argument; I was just starving for information. I wanted a deeper understanding of the world and its workings, and loved when elders would explain things to me in detail. I gravitated to people who would take the time to tell me what they knew. Sometimes they found me exhausting, to the point where they'd tell me to bugger off. You see, in my culture, children weren't supposed to question their elders. They were supposed to be seen and not heard. So, it was a bit of a shock to my dad or uncles when I peppered them with endless questions. I remember some of my dad's friends saying, "Man, what's up with this kid?" They weren't being disrespectful; they were just marvelling at how much of an anomaly I was. "Boi, yuh ask a lot of questions, yuh know," they'd remark with a smile.

I guess it all worked to my benefit, though. In grade six, I wrote the Common Entrance Exam and placed in the 99th percentile on the island. Because of that, when I was ten I received an academic scholarship to Knox College high school, in Clarendon, the parish next to Manchester.

Books were fine, but I relished spending time under the beautiful Jamaican sun. I played with my friends and brothers and their friends, too. Whenever I got a pair of new running shoes, I would leave them in the box and go play outside in bare feet. There was a little game we devised with a few big bicycle tires that we pushed down a hill. A couple boys would set up the tires and the others would run behind, trying to overtake the speeding rubber. We made our own toys. My dad once brought home a table hockey game from this far-off country, but my spirit didn't take to it. I vividly remember thinking, *What the hell is this?* I was told that's what children play with in Canada.

I didn't get it. All I knew of that country was that it had snow. We used to get Christmas cards from family who lived there, and I remember thinking it must be warm in that country, because in the pictures, people were always playing out in the snow, which looked like cotton balls. If people were outside and lying in the snow, making these things they called "snow angels," why would I even think to associate snow with cold? It just didn't make any sense to me that someone might lie in something that is freezing.

We didn't have a television for many years, so it was books and radio that connected us to the world outside of Manchester. My grandfather owned a little black radio, probably about five inches wide, with two little knobs and a red dial that switched between three stations. He always had it turned on, blasting reggae, church programming, news or sports. There was a vibrancy that emanated from the radio, an incredible liveliness that I really enjoyed. Something was always happening somewhere in the world, and hearing about it served to stimulate my active mind and keep me on the edge of my seat. My grandfather listened to cricket and boxing and, of course, track and field. But meets weren't broadcast every week as they are today, just the marquee events. Back then, the Pan American Games and the Commonwealth Games were massive in Jamaica, as well as the Olympics, obviously. The World Athletics Championships weren't in existence yet. Listening to the feats of my countrymen Donald Quarrie and Lennox Miller, or the great Cuban runner Alberto Juantorena, enthralled me. I would hear the broadcaster say during a competition, "And on the back stretch," and it was almost like they were describing a horse—a beautiful being born with majestic speed. That excited the hell out of me.

I wasn't aspiring to be like them at the time, but listening to broadcasts of their competitions offered me pure joy. I would listen and think it must be so much fun to be part of that, to be the person providing such incredible entertainment and satisfaction for this whole slew of people. When we'd hear that Donald Quarrie was about to sprint, the whole village and all the people who were working on our farm would come and huddle in front of one little radio. Track and field was appointment listening.

Cricket—another remnant of the British—was a big draw, too. The guys at the rum shop would keep it on in the background as they played dominoes, but the matches were frequent and long, and nobody felt the need to observe every batsman. Instead, conversation would stray, usually to politics.

Politics can be quite consuming in the Caribbean. There are often distinct lines drawn between supporters of the various parties, and that can cause all kinds of friction and fighting. In some countries, it can even lead to murder. Sports tended to provide unification. Even if two people resided on opposite ends of the political spectrum, they could sit together peacefully if their favourite athlete or team was competing. That environment shaped the value I put on sport. I learned to view it as more than just games and athletic triumphs. It was a conduit that could spread real joy and bring people together. Two people who hated each other could listen to a broadcast of their country's sprinter, then look up, say, "Ah, good one. Until next time," and go peacefully on their separate ways.

For all the sprinters and batsmen that drew our village, farm and family to the radio, my young ear tuned in most acutely to a singular athlete, one who was not a track star but who wielded a special power to unite people. My grandfather would play Muhammad Ali's boxing matches on the radio in the early 1970s, and those fights were mesmerizing. But more than Ali's bouts, I gravitated to his interviews. His voice and the way he communicated was simply magnetic, and the unabashed self-confidence he exuded every time a microphone was placed in front of him resonated with me deeply.

If you're not familiar with West Indian culture, then I'll put it simply: we do not lack self-confidence. This is especially true for Jamaican men. Whether it's the environment we grew up in or the survival instincts developed by our ancestors who were enslaved or hired as indentured labourers by the British, the end result is that we tend to be self-assured. This confidence can be perceived negatively outside our culture—but I'll get to that later. When I was a boy listening to Ali talk about how pretty he was or brazenly dissect his dominance over an opponent, I felt that I understood him on a deeper level. He was free as a human being, and observing that left an imprint on me. I realized, even back then, that he felt a responsibility to drive forward a generation of people in the United States. There was—and still is—baggage from slavery in that country, and he was trying to help shed some of it and demonstrate that you can be good-looking, uncompromising, successful and Black at the same time.

I have always been struck by how the subjects of race and slavery sit differently in the mindsets of Black people from

North America and those from the Caribbean. It's as if an inter-generational trauma exists in Canada and the States that we don't have in Jamaica. In my own experience, there was a different level of thought about who I was—I was, simply, Jamaican. I wasn't called a Black-Jamaican. I was Jamaican. Do you see the difference? I grew up embracing that straightforward sense of identity with confidence, and was surrounded predominantly by people who looked like me and shared my experience. I know that my Black friends who were born and raised in North America had a totally different experience. They were minorities where they lived, and they weren't always accepted. I never walked into a room thinking, *I'm a Black guy*. I know that's a privilege that was afforded to me because of where I grew up. And my environment influenced my mindset. Back home, we owned land. Because of that, I didn't have to contemplate how life had been different in Africa generations ago. I knew my grandparents and parents as landowners and employers.

The diversity of my own family also informed my thinking. While I identify as Black, my DNA is the product of the colonial past and contains traces from across the globe. My mother had East Indian and Maroon influences in her ancestry, while my father's line traced back to Ireland, Asia and Africa. I never needed to take a 23andMe genetic test to understand the complexity of my family history. I could look around at a family gathering and see evidence of all the places we had come from. Walk through the door and you'll see someone who looks like they're from Norway, another who looks like they're from India, and they would be chatting with someone who looks Cameroonian. I remember bringing a white Canadian to a family reunion in Jamaica, and he was like, "What the hell—that's your cousin? Seriously?" I have Jamaican family members who have been mistaken for being Scottish or Chinese. That kind of diversity has always been very normal to me, and I know it to be the case for many people from Jamaica and across the Caribbean.

That big extended family played a vital role in my childhood, and there was one member of it in particular who was a mighty pillar in my support system: my Uncle Keith. He was my mother's younger brother and was very close to her. He didn't live in Jamaica, but he was only a short flight away, in Florida, and he'd visit us quite often. As soon as Uncle Keith touched down in Kingston, he'd make a beeline for Manchester, always bearing gifts—church shoes, T-shirts, or even cash. He was among the most generous people I've ever met in my life, and whenever he handed me ten bucks, I felt like the richest kid on the island.

Uncle Keith was an adult I could bare my soul to in conversation. Just like my father would dictate to me, Uncle Keith did not discuss or debate with his children. However, I wasn't his child, and that allowed us to build a unique kinship. I could get away with a bit more with him than I ever could at home.

When he took me out for soda, ice cream or candy, we'd chat about what was going on in my life—girlfriends, sports, school and everything in between. He offered wonderful advice to me, and by the time I was in elementary school, I loved every moment I got to spend with him. Uncle Keith had a Honda Super Cub motorcycle and would stick me on the bike with him, no helmet, and take me around Manchester to visit other family members. He'd stop in at a rum shop or two along the route and have a couple drinks with his friends. He'd hand me a bottle of Coke and grab me a stool so I could sit by the bar and hang out with them. I wasn't quite as bold with peppering Uncle Keith's friends with questions, but I remained observant and listened intently as they gaffed about sports and politics. The upcoming cricket match or elections would elicit spirited conversations from them, and I soaked it all in. It used to make me feel like such a big guy. My dad would never allow me to do that. Oh, hell no. Father and son going to a rum shop would be unthinkable for Mr. Bailey.

The first time my feet ever touched a track, I was five years old. It was Sports Day at school, and track and field was the main draw. To this day, I firmly believe that track is the best sport in the world for building self-esteem in children, because anyone—big, skinny, short, tall—can find an event that suits their strengths. Some kids are better at throwing, while others might have the vertical lift to be a pole vaulter or long-jumper. I learned, right from day one at school, that those activities weren't for me.

I was blessed with speed.

On my first Sports Day, when I was just starting school, I was wearing running shoes that my parents had recently bought me. They were neat and clean and carefully preserved. I had taken great efforts in the previous weeks to avoid wearing them so as not to scuff them up ahead of Sports Day. Whenever I played outside with my brothers and friends, I went barefoot rather than risk anything happening to those shoes. I always wondered whether those years of sprinting barefoot as a kid better positioned my body for my career path. Later in life, I realized it had done exactly that. Running barefoot had provided a direct connection from my brain to the muscles in my legs and feet. When I became a professional athlete, I would always make a point of taking my shoes off during training and walking on the grass. It would help me be in touch with the soles of my feet and ensure I was moving with the correct heel-to-toe form.

My first activity on Sports Day was the 100-metre dash. As I stepped onto the grass track, I noticed markings made by white limestone. These marks distinguished the lanes we'd race in, two feet wide for the entire length of the runway. I could never have known how much of my life those few steps would serve to foreshadow. In that moment, it just felt like everything was right in the world. Once the starting whistle blew, I leaped off the mark. I'd had no training at that age—I was barely old enough for school—yet sprinting felt natural to me. I felt free on the track. Sprinting at full speed, I sometimes wonder if this is what a bird feels like as it soars through the sky. It's a distinct sense of freedom that's been present in my life ever since I first felt it on that grass track in Jamaica. When I reached the end of the 100 metres and that feeling came to an end, I realized none of the other boys were near me. I had smoked the competition.

Winning wasn't bad. In addition to the endorphins, dominating the 100-metre event on Sports Day brought me adulation from students and teachers. I relished these spoils of victory. My mom and dad, on the other hand, didn't care much for the distraction.

"That's good, son, but how'd you do on your test?"

My parents weren't unsupportive of my growing interest in athletics, but for them, sports came after school. Every time I came home with good news from the track, the conversation quickly circled back to academics.

Competition was teaching me more than the thrills of victory. It also brought my first exposure to failure. Now, I should couch that by saying my mother taught us there was no such thing as failure, per se. She had a mantra for those moments when we didn't get something we wanted: "It's not your time." She always used that phrase, and I think it provided us with a beautiful outlook. "It's not your time" can mean you're not ready in life for something to come to you or even that you're just not *prepared* to make it happen. It can also ensure you're not driving yourself crazy with regret.

By age ten, I was very active in track. I used to jog past Mount Olivet Public School, waving to the students and teachers watching from the windows, as I made my way to track meets in Spaldings, home of my future high school. In my last year before moving to Canada, I competed in one of Jamaica's signature sporting events, the Inter-Secondary Schools Boys and Girls Championships—affectionately known as Champs. It's a huge event, with high schools from across the country sending their best athletes to compete in a week-long track meet. It is the place to see the talent likely to challenge for Olympic gold in just a few more years. If you'd attended in 2003, you'd have witnessed a teenage Usain Bolt announce his impending dominance in front of 30,000 fans under the bright lights of the National Stadium in Kingston. And if you'd been lucky enough to have a ticket in 1978, you could have watched me in the 100-metre and 4x100 relay finals, representing Knox College. My high school wasn't a big sports school; we were known for academics. So a Knox student making the finals in two categories at Champs was an accomplishment worth noticing.

At Champs I was expecting to win, as increasingly I did. However, in the hours before competition I got nervous about competing at such a high level and I ate a half-ripe banana that gave me a serious bout of diarrhea. I still mustered the energy to sprint but finished fifth (in class four, and fourth in the relay). Naturally, I was pissed off and disappointed in myself. But as my anger faded, I could hear my mom's voice in my head saying, "That's horrible, but it's just not your time." She was right. Not even future champions win every race, so you'd better learn to handle yourself when you lose. My mother gave me the tools to do that.

My mom was full of wisdom, and sometimes she delivered her wisdom complete with a scalp massage. It always helped. Like the time we were sitting together in the bus travelling through the Jamaican countryside when her eyes began to glisten. The reason for those tears—so uncommon for my mother—was our destination. Or, I should say, my destination. We were making the roughly 100-kilometre drive from Manchester Parish to the airport in Kingston.

I was moving to Canada.

By this time, my father had been working there as a machinist for a number of years. He came back to Jamaica to visit whenever he could, and I went to Canada one summer to visit, but he was up north to stay, and he had already brought O'Neil north to live with him. Life in Canada could provide a better post-secondary education and would allow for greater opportunities after graduation. My mother accepted that, no matter how hard of a pill it was to swallow, watching her boys leave. But she had decided to remain in Jamaica. That country up north was too cold. My dad could handle it, but, physically, my mother just could not. She also hated travelling. Even later in life, when I became the greatest sprinter in the world, she declined offers of a private plane to watch me compete. "After you win, come home so we can sit down and I can make you a meal," she would tell me (I always took her up on the offer). Being in Jamaica just felt right to her. She preferred her *own* surroundings—it's where her family had always been and where she had control over her household and life. My mom didn't even like the cities of Kingston and Mandeville. Basically, she hated any place that was not her own tiny enclave, where she could go for a walk and have tea at her neighbour's house. Canada was out of the question.

After my father had lived in Canada for some time, my parents' relationship had run its course. They split up. They'd never actually been married. My dad did finally marry a woman he met in Canada, named Icilda, and my mother eventually married a man I referred to as Mr. Lewis, in Jamaica. There was never any animosity between my parents after they split. In retrospect, they maintained an incredible relationship and always put the well-being of their children first. No matter which country I was in, I was always surrounded by my mother and father, one in person and one on the phone, plus two bonus step-parents.

In the early 1970s, my father had worked in Jamaica for a company named Alcan. As a machinist, he was a blue-collar guy who wasn't afraid of the grind. He could stand on his feet for twelve hours a day in a factory and never complain. That skill set led him to a job opportunity in Canada, and he seized on it. He moved to a town in Ontario called Oakville and would send money back home to my mother along with letters for his sons. Even after they split up, anytime he could squeeze in a trip on vacation time, he'd be right back on the farm with us.

This was the case for several years. However, when I was twelve, it was time for me to join my father and O'Neil. Unlike my previous visits to Oakville, this was a permanent move. And so, on that trip to the airport with my mother, for the first time in my entire life, I witnessed her cry sad tears. I could not fully comprehend the emotions she was feeling in that moment, but I knew something deep was happening there. She was no longer going to be able to see her son every morning and wouldn't be able to converse and laugh with him after school, or feed him— an act she cherished. To her credit, even while she was staring down this new reality, Daisy was also happy. She knew this was the right step, and that it would open a plethora of doors for me.

My mother's selflessness still touches me to this day. She knew that finishing high school in Canada while living with my father and new stepmother was ultimately the right thing for my future. She sacrificed her own happiness so I could enjoy greater opportunity, and that sacrifice—as little as I might have understood it at twelve years old—became something I carried with me as I grew up.

CHAPTER 2

O'NEIL'S LITTLE BROTHER IS HERE

THE FIRST TIME I stepped foot in Canada, I was seven. My father had always said that I would eventually join him in Oakville, so even before my first visit, I made sure to study up on the country. I went to the library near our home in Manchester and borrowed as many books about Canada as I could find. I read about hockey and ice-skating and Niagara Falls. I learned about the weather up there. It looked very different than what we had in Jamaica.

Canada always seemed to me to be a country with endless pos-
sibilities for the people who resided there. That initial summer
visit was also my first experience on a plane. But I had also read
about planes and knew what to expect. Even though I flew
alone at seven years old, I wasn't too nervous. After I landed
and my dad took me to his house in Oakville, I began to observe things that I'd seen in the books. Studying had given me
a sense of familiarity with my future home, and seeing it now in
person was almost like I was no longer reading about the world
beyond Jamaica's shores but participating in it.

That sensation was very much alive when my dad took me
to Niagara Falls. I had read that it is one of the wonders of the
world, and it did not disappoint. I lived among mountains in
Jamaica and would occasionally go to a beach, any of which
were beautiful. This, however, was majestic. As I stood gaping
at the thundering falls, they seemed out of this world. The
massive crowds of bustling tourists that seemed to have gathered from all over the world only added to the spectacle's gran-
deur. To be in Canada was like a window opening, a window
that looked out onto the rest of the world. Suddenly, it was all
real and within reach. As far as I was concerned, my quiet farm
life was now firmly in the rear-view mirror.

But I was still a child and in my father's care. Around that time,
he had started a community organization in Oakville called
the Canadian Caribbean Association of Halton (CCA). Its gatherings brought Caribbean expats together and allowed them to
widen their business and personal networks. Our trip to Niagara
Falls had been planned by the organization, which was really a
giant melting pot of people. It drew together members from

the entire Caribbean diaspora—Jamaica, Trinidad and Guyana, among other places. Some people had even married white Canadians, and the connections made by members proved very fruitful. As an added bonus, the event served West Indian food, as their events always did. Someone would inevitably whip up meals of rice and peas to go along with oxtail, jerk chicken or curry goat, and toss them in a cooler. It helped provide a taste of home, because the food in Canada was quite different. In the 1970s, international cuisine of most kinds was much harder to find than it is today.

After several weeks in Oakville, I flew back to Jamaica with a sense of what my life could one day entail, were I to live in Canada. But as with any child, thoughts of the future were pushed aside by the present. My mom, my friends and my school were in Manchester. Life resumed almost seamlessly for me and, aside from a couple more summer trips to stay with my father, it remained as I'd always known it for the next five years.

Then came August 21, 1980. I got dressed to the nines in my light brown, three-piece suit and matching boots. My move to Canada was finally happening, and as I looked in the mirror at my twelve-year-old self, I felt like the king of the world. I wanted my new countrymen and -women to think, *This guy has style*, as soon as I touched down at the airport in Toronto. My dad picked me up and brought me to his new house in Oakville, and my new life was officially underway. The detached house was situated on a tranquil suburban street and had its own two-car garage and a long driveway that could fit a few more vehicles. The only sign of nature was a big tree that grew in the middle of a decent-sized lawn, making it very different than our farm in Jamaica. Also, our neighbours' house was only a few feet away, which took some getting used to.

In the garage, I found something special waiting for me: a bike. It was a hand-me-down from O'Neil, but I treated it as if I'd inherited my own Ferrari. I had never had a bike, so I made it my mission to get right on and learn how to ride it. Those two wheels represented my first mode of transportation and my first means to independence. I was a quick learner and twelve years old, so there was no way I was using training wheels. Of course, I fell and scratched my knees a couple of times. But I got the hang of it, and soon enough, I could ride it anywhere and visit all my new friends in the neighbourhood. It seemed as if I had been living in the neighbourhood all my life.

My two eldest brothers, Glenroy and Wilburn, didn't come to Canada to join my father. They were much older and already semi-established back home, so it didn't make sense for them to relocate. But O'Neil was just fourteen years old, and having him around made my acclimatization easier. He was a high-school sports superstar. Man, he was a hotshot. He excelled at everything he touched, whether it was long jump, basketball, football, you name it. His success prepared a seat at the table for me—it was almost like he laid out the plates and cutlery so that I could eat. Older students welcomed me because of him: "O'Neil's little brother is here!" I never worried about fitting in.

Life in my new neighbourhood on Woburn Crescent was idyllic. It was working class and suburban, with nicely manicured lawns and trees dotting the entire street, and the houses were relatively new, probably just a decade old. It being Canada, the kids were constantly out on the street playing road hockey, although pickup basketball always stole my attention away. I felt immense pride when I helped my dad put up a handmade number sign on the front of our house, above the garage. That bonding activity was his way of helping me plant my very own flag on my new life.

The neighbourhood made it easy to feel at home. There was plenty of diversity in that area of Oakville, more than you would expect during the early 1980s. A Chinese-Trinidadian family lived across the street from me. My neighbours were Portuguese, Italian and Yugoslavian. There were a few Black families, and my best friend, Rick Baptiste, was Afro-Guyanese. Donald Wilson and Warren Chase were also of Caribbean descent, and other buddies hailed from Barbados, St. Lucia and even India. Many of us were new to Canada, or our parents had been, and that served as a bonding agent for our friendships. There were also kids whose families had been in Ontario for generations. They embraced us as friends and neighbours, and there was a shared understanding that all of our parents were working their asses off and wanted to create a strong and safe neighbourhood.

Being surrounded by that type of diversity gave me a high level of comfort growing up. I didn't experience racism in the same way that Black people in other Canadian communities might have. We were a group of boys and supported each other. And we had an understanding that if you messed with me, started some shit or slung a racial epithet my way, then you would have to deal with the repercussions from *all of us*, including my white friends.

It was never lost on me that we lived in a *house*. I've always been grateful for that. Plenty of immigrants never had that kind of space or comfort. I don't know what my dad had to pay for that house, but he made it work. Both my parents sacrificed to ensure their children had the chance to build successful futures, and their commitment to us was steadfast. As part of that, my father made sure I had a strong understanding of fiscal responsibility. He took me to the CIBC at Hopedale Mall the year after I arrived from Jamaica and educated me about mortgages. I was only twelve!

I came to understand that it was harder for him, as a Black man, to obtain a mortgage from banks than it was for some of his white friends. He wasn't bothered, though, and said to himself, *I want a house. So, if I need to work eighteen hours a day to get a proper house in a proper neighbourhood where my kids can go to school and get a great education and an amazing start in life—better than I had—then I'm going to do whatever it is I need to do.* He certainly delivered on that promise. I remember my father took us all out to a fancy restaurant when he learned that his mortgage rate had been reduced to 13.25 from 19.75 percent. It was at the Omega restaurant, and anyone from Oakville will tell you that it was the biggest and best steakhouse in the community. Maybe it didn't dawn on me at that age, but that dinner helped me understand what a mortgage is and how its parameters could be a difference-maker in your life.

As a boy, I spent a lot of quality time with my father, and one of our favourite shared activities was watching boxing. In Jamaica, I had listened to Muhammad Ali's fights on the radio, and now I was able to observe his greatness on television. Watching his in-ring performances, though, was almost secondary to his interviews. I loved Ali's press conferences and interviews with broadcasters like Howard Cosell. It was as if he were giving a master class in how to conduct yourself with his tailored suits, clean-shaven face and charismatic and engaging verbiage. I wanted to emulate him, not only as a man who believed in himself, but one who looked the part, too. I had seen pictures of him before I saw him on TV, but those were mostly black-and-white newspaper clippings. Seeing him on screen in colour was a different story. I noticed the way that Ali moved with what looked to my young eyes like thousands of reporters and people hanging on to his every word. He was also—and this meant a great deal to me—a *powerful, confident Black* man.

I've always respected the need for young people to have role models who look like them. It's vitally important for people to see themselves in movies, on TV and at sporting venues. In Western countries, that's always been a given for white people. But for most others, those role models haven't been there nearly so often, and that can lead to all kinds of internal struggle and trauma. How can you believe you can be something when you grow up without seeing someone else in that role? How can you believe you can do something when you're conditioned to think it's impossible? For me, Ali was the antidote to all that. Ali exemplified for me that greatness was possible.

While I was blossoming as a young person in Oakville, I began to really miss my mom. Being away from her, especially in the early days, was hard. I called her as often as I could and feverishly wrote letters to her. Dad cared deeply for us, but she was the one person I could completely confide in—a soft place where I could land and escape any hardships that life brought my way. People always ask me how I looked after my mental health during my career and if I worked with any sports psychologists along the way. I tell them, "No, my mother filled that role in my life." She was the one who talked with me about my goals and plans. She was the one who asked how I felt when it was clear I needed a sympathetic ear. I fully trusted that I was going to receive support no matter what I revealed to her. While my dad might dismiss my uncertainties with a curt "That's just stupid" or "Stop being that way," my mom would ask, "What are your thoughts?" I never hesitated to reveal my deeper emotions to her.

That I held my mother in such esteem did not help me get along with my stepmother. I bristled against the thought that she was trying to replace my mom. I realize now that I was being headstrong, but I wrote to my mother and told her exactly how I felt. She told me not to worry, I'd be fine. If I just stayed focused on school everything would work out.

I had appreciated the approach that my stepfather, Clarence, had taken toward me. He told me, during our very first conversation, "Hey, I'm going to get married to your mother. I just want to let you know that I am not your father. In fact, your father and I are going to have many conversations, but I just want you to know that I'm the man of the house. Whatever rules that have been laid down, I am going to make sure that it stays that way." I respected that. He made it clear that he was not going to replace my dad, but neither was I. We came to a quick understanding. It just wasn't that way with my stepmother, though.

Like many teenage boys, I was always thinking about girls. I was calling girlfriends on the phone and spitting lyrics from

Teddy Pendergrass and Luther Vandross songs to try to impress them. Slow jams were my thing back then. I found it a nice way to balance the aggressive, competitive demeanour I carried toward sports. Icilda didn't like that I was tying up the phone and would ask me to get off—remember, in those days, most houses had only a single land line. I viewed that as her cramping my style. I also didn't like the curfews and other rules she put in place, and so, to maintain my sense of freedom and get away from that element at home, I threw myself into sports.

I attended high school at Queen Elizabeth Park, which had a modest track made of black asphalt. There was a little bit of a buzz around the school when I arrived because of the reputation that O'Neil had built on that exact runway. He was a dominant sprinter, and classmates were wondering if his little brother could run like he did.

That was a given.

Sprinting still came very easily to me, even though I didn't get any real training at the high-school level. I was actually cut from the team each year because I didn't attend practices. Those sessions took place at 7:30 a.m., and during the spring in Ontario, mornings can be pretty chilly. I absolutely hated the cold and routinely skipped those practices, starting a sort of cat-and-mouse game with the coaches.

Thankfully, I could depend on a couple of good friends to alert me to when the team was holding run-offs in practice to determine who would make the team ahead of regional meets. O'Neil did that, too, during the time when my high-school years overlapped with his. A common refrain among our track coaches was "Oh, the Bailey brothers again? God help us." It's tough for me to evaluate the quality of our high-school track program compared to others in the region, simply because I hadn't yet learned to respect the sport. However, I will say that all the athletic coaches I encountered at Queen Elizabeth Park were stand-up men. Their care for us extended beyond sports. They were concerned about our grades and worked to help us develop manners and etiquette that would benefit us later in life. Paul Roper was my main track coach in high school, and over the years, we've shared many laughs about my exploits. His favourite line goes something like this: "I'm the only track coach in the history of the world to cut the fastest man in history."

The accolades were pouring in steadily for me: Halton Region 100-metre champion, long jump champion, relay champion. O'Neil had set a bunch of school records, and by the time I graduated from Queen Elizabeth Park, each of those belonged to me. Despite that wild success, track and field was just an extracurricular activity for me, something I participated in to get out of the house and nearer to my friends. As a sport, sprinting was failing to capture my heart in the way another sport had already done.

I had had zero exposure to basketball while living in Jamaica. The closest hint of the sport was the rims used for netball, which was predominantly played by women. When I arrived in Oakville and O'Neil introduced me to basketball, I quickly fell in love. The camaraderie and team aspect of the sport really enticed me. Football offered those same features, and I gave that sport a try in high school, too. But I was done with football after one practice. It was cold out on the field, and I saw guys tackling each other. I said, "You're trying to kill each other for the ball? And it's freezing outside? You can have the ball. I'm good." To this day, I find football an amazing sport to watch, but basketball was my style. It was more graceful—an artful blend of skills and explosive power. And, let's not forget, basketball could be played indoors, which, for a kid still only a few years out of the sunny Caribbean, counted for a lot.

I made the midget basketball team in my first year at Queen Elizabeth Park. I was definitely a work in progress for the coaches. I was the best overall athlete on the floor, but I could not handle the ball and dribbled by slapping it forcefully. Our point guard, John, used to call me "Stone Hands," and would jokingly say, "I can't pass to Stone Hands." I was around five-foot-seven at the time, but I could jump. Even at age twelve, I could grab the rim when I leaped with some momentum. My first dunk came in a game against Milton that year, too.

There were probably 100 spectators in our small gymnasium during the Halton championships, but to me it felt like 1,000. My teammate took a shot that rattled around the rim without going in. I spotted my chance. I barely caught the rebound with my fingertips amidst a flurry of defenders, but within a split second, I managed to gather a bit of momentum, leaped as high as I could and attacked the rim. The audience erupted, and I'll never forget the sound of their cheers reverberating off the gym walls. The momentum of the game shifted, and we ended up securing the championship. Afterwards, people said to me, "Oh my God. How did you get up that high?" That dunk was a proud moment that not only emboldened my love for basketball but also introduced me to the thrill of wowing a large crowd with athletic feats.

I give a lot of credit to my midget basketball coach, Gary Gregson. He is one of the nicest people I've ever come across. He knew I was stronger, faster and more athletic than any of the other twelve-year-olds but needed to be taught how to play the game. He took on that responsibility and helped me develop the finer skills, like how to guard an offensive player. I loved defence. My body was built for it. I had a fifty-inch vertical leap and could move quicker than anyone, forward, backward and laterally. And the defensive side of the game didn't require me to dribble the ball or shoot, which I wasn't very good at yet. While those skills slowly developed, my defence allowed me to contribute to the squad in a meaningful way. It also helped that I was fearless on the court. It didn't matter who I was guarding, even if the ball-handler towered over me, everyone knew I wasn't going to back down.

I surrounded myself with basketball in high school. I could play pickup with my friends, practice and take part in games with my team, and then go home at the end of the day and watch NBA games. In the same way that I looked up to Ali, I began to find my basketball heroes. Utah Jazz shooting guard Darrell Griffith was among my favourites, as well as Philadelphia 76ers centre Darryl Dawkins. But the man who really captured my attention and imagination was Atlanta Hawks star Dominique Wilkins. He was known for his acrobatic slam dunks and earned the nickname "The Human Highlight Film." As my love for basketball grew, I looked up to him more and more. I loved the way Michael Jordan played, but I always preferred Wilkins because that's who I wanted to be. I aspired to be the guy who could back you up in the key and drop step dunk right in your face. I desperately wanted to be a six-foot-eight power forward in the NBA.

There was no push and pull between track and basketball in my life. Basketball dominated. Truthfully, it still does. Sprinting came naturally to me. There wasn't any thought or deep struggle associated with learning how to do it. I would just lace up my spikes, warm my body up a bit and crush the competition. I was born for that. Basketball represented a greater challenge. My body gifted me the ability to be a good guard and dunker, but the finer elements of the sport required great effort, study and concentration. I had to work hard to be good at it, and I think that's the reason basketball captured my heart in ways track and field never could.

When my friends and I skipped class, we weren't going to the movie theatre or the mall. We went to the gym and practised our dribbling, shooting and dunking. We skipped school to stay in school. The coaches knew they would find us there and would often poke their heads in and yell, "Guys, you know there's a class going on right now?" They would be pissed off with us, and our social studies and math teachers would be even more upset. But I loved the sport and was determined to improve. I topped out at six foot two, and because of my late introduction to the game, going to the NBA was likely an unrealistic goal. No scouts were crossing the border to watch me play. But those thoughts didn't enter my head. I figured I still had a shot.

I believe you have to think that way in life. A thought has driven me for my entire career, from sprinting through my later accomplishments: "I can do this. Why not me?" It wasn't even the money associated with playing professional basketball appealing to my teenage ambition. I would have played the game for a bag of frickin' ice cubes.

Basketball also opened my mind to the possibility of helping others. When my buddies and I would play pickup games at the local YMCA, we'd come across kids involved with the Oakville chapter of the Big Brothers organization. Some were our age, some a little younger or older. But they were mostly from single-parent households, and the organization leaders and some of the adults around the Y realized it was good for these kids to spend time with us. The adults would always ask if we would be there to play pickup when the Big Brothers kids were coming. I had an incredible support system and figured that if there was any way I could help these youth, whom I had taken a liking to, then it would be worth my time. Rick would join me. We'd ride our bikes over together and meet up with the kids on the court.

Even then, at seventeen years of age, I was able to pick up on people's mannerisms and decipher what they meant. When it comes to children, you can read a lot from their eyes. If you motivate them or stimulate their mind, their eyes tend to display a certain sparkle. They light up, so to speak. When Rick and I showed up at the YMCA, or sometimes the Oaklands Regional Centre, to hoop with those youth, I saw that sparkle in their eyes. They were so grateful that we were there. They needed it.

Basketball wasn't going to open professional opportunities for me, but track and field was giving me options. I received several track scholarship offers from colleges in the United States as I was nearing high-school graduation. Syracuse University, Western

Texas College and Central State in Ohio were among those that came calling. I was just seventeen years old at the time, though, and my father stepped in and stopped me from accepting any such offer. He felt that I wasn't mature enough yet to handle life on my own at an American college. I know he wasn't being malicious, undermining my ambition. Not at all. He was just very protective. His plan was for me to live at home while attending Sheridan College, which had a campus just down the road in Oakville.

Later in life, I accepted his reasoning. At seventeen, I was simply not in the right frame of mind to move to the U.S. to compete in track and field and succeed. I don't think any coach or program could have got through to me at that stage in life. I was not prepared mentally or physically to succeed at that level in the sport. In the moment, though, I was upset. I knew my father's decision was final. But it's human nature for any strong-minded teenager to rail against the fact that you're not yet in complete control of your life. I didn't talk back to him—I've never done that with my father. It was too engrained in me as a child that what our parents say goes, without question. But not pushing back didn't mean I wasn't disappointed.

I wrote to my mother to explain my father's decision and how I felt about it: "There were academic opportunities tied to track and field for me in America, but Dad doesn't think I'm ready for this, and I'm not happy about that." Even though my mother and father weren't a couple, they communicated with each other every day throughout the rest of their lives, and their kids' success was always paramount to them. My mother agreed with my dad that I wasn't ready, but she heard me out and shared with him how I felt. My father approached me one day to talk about it. I'll never know what she said to him or whether she tried to convince him to change his mind, but his message to me was as clear as ever.

"I spoke to your mom. I still don't think that you're ready."

And that was that.

CHAPTER 3

THE UNEXPECTED RETURN

I WASN'T GOING TO be a college track star in the U.S., and more disappointingly, the NBA still hadn't come calling. But someone did, and he was giving me a chance to play the game I loved most.

During my senior year of high school, Wayne Allison, who coached the basketball team at Sheridan, recruited me to join the varsity Bruins. Several local colleges and universities had tried to recruit me, but Wayne was familiar with me because our high-school basketball team would compete in tournaments at the Sheridan gym. He'd send a scout to watch us or sometimes swing by himself. One conversation with him particularly stands out to me: he told me that he wanted to work with me because I was a "project."

"Listen, man, you got all the tools," Wayne said. "But you need some more work."

He was right. I couldn't dribble or shoot the ball as well as I could have. However, Wayne also conveyed to me that I was the best raw athlete on the court and that he wanted to maximize my talent. That was all I needed to hear.

The idea of being a project appealed to me. And as you will learn later in this book, there's a throughline between that and my relationship with coaches. Because of the way I was raised, specifically due to the rules set out by my father, I love structure. I need a structured environment and a concrete plan to really succeed. I'm obsessive in that way and believe in perfection. So, Wayne coming to me and saying that I could be his project let me know that he had already put serious thought into how I could evolve on the court. He had a plan, and he was willing to invest his time and resources into making me better.

That lit a fire in me. Wayne's trust helped ease the sting of my dad's decision. If I was going to miss out on the glory of a college track career, at least I'd be playing basketball. That was no small consolation prize. The days when I was referred to as "Stone Hands" were long gone. I had blossomed into a productive power forward at six-foot-two with a fifty-inch vertical leap. I wasn't the best player on the college squad—I'd score a few points every night—but people really came to watch me play because of the athleticism and excitement that I brought to each game. When I was on the Sheridan court, I was always able to make something happen; that could be a monster dunk on one night, or sparkling defence that spurred fast break transitions on another night. I absolutely cherished my time on that basketball team.

I cherished my time at Sheridan in general. It just felt like an extension of high school. And that meant I kept some of my habits—good and bad—from Queen Elizabeth Park. I was still a gym rat who would spend countless hours practising with my friends. But teachers weren't scolding us for skipping class. Nobody really cared if I didn't attend a lecture. I studied business administration and economics and, just like at previous points in my life, the school work was not challenging to me. I could easily get the marks I needed to get by. Basketball was where I sought to make the most improvement.

Wayne proved to be an excellent coach. His communication skills were elite, and he spoke with authority and could be frank about everyone's strengths and weaknesses while keeping us motivated to improve. I respected people who did that. Wayne had played the game at a high level, and he was a big man who spoke firmly but never relied on his size to intimidate and get his way. His players trusted what he said because he was constantly putting in the work to develop himself as a coach, and that would show up when he devised new plays or drills for our team. His record speaks for itself, too. Wayne compiled an overall record of 332-200 during his coaching career while winning 70 percent of his Ontario Colleges Athletic Association conference games (188-82).

Most games, I came off the bench as the sixth man. But that didn't stop thoughts of a future in basketball from creeping into my head. There were times when I felt success at Sheridan might be my ticket to going pro. If I ever got upset with not receiving more minutes as a starter, I would think back to my mother's sage advice: "It's not your time." I could be sitting on the bench during the opening tip-off and not have one ounce of discouragement in my soul. I'd just think, *I'll get my moment. It's just not now. Soon the scouts will show up in droves to see me. My time will come.*

While that might have been far-fetched, there were occasions that emboldened my resolve. Wayne had listed my height in our college program as six-foot-six, which was generous by a good five inches. I don't know if that was a typo on his part or mind games with the opposition. I think he wanted other schools to perceive the Bruins as a team with intimidating size. I'll never forget that during our championship run, Coach sent me on the court in one game to guard a six-foot-eight player—a hulking white guy from northern Alberta. When he saw me walk onto the court, he burst out laughing. "You're not six-foot-six," he exclaimed. I shrugged him off, and when the whistle blew, I made sure to stick to him like a barnacle. He caught a pass from a teammate in the offensive zone and took a few dribbles with me on his back. He spun and tried for a turnaround jumper. I knew that was coming and jumped as high as I could, blocking his shot with two hands and snatching the ball out of the air. Those seven inches he had on me didn't matter, and I made sure to let him know that. "Yeah, I'm not six-six," I yelled. "Let's fucking go!" A little later in the same game, our point guard Bruce

Nelson was leading a fast break down the court and spotted me on the right wing. He knew exactly where my head was at and lobbed a high pass toward the net, just above the same guy. Before the big Albertan realized I was there, I had slammed the alley-oop while jumping over his head. Picture the famous Vince Carter posterization during the 2000 Olympics. It was *that* vicious. Definitely a highlight in my basketball career.

The spirit of competition has always driven me to great lengths. It provides me with this rush of adrenalin that's hard to describe. There's nothing like it. But being seriously competitive means practising, and though I loved my gym time, I felt very differently about long days at the track.

Once I had graduated from high school, track and field was no longer a constant in my life. Sheridan didn't have a track team, and I had mostly separated myself from sprinting. I was fine with never again having a track coach run me through drills that I viewed as boring and tedious. The A and B skips were the worst. They were pre-acceleration drills designed to instill muscle memory in your body, while at the same time honing a technique that breeds efficiency in movement. You might have done some of these during your phys-ed classes in school. For A skips, the movement requires you to stay upright and tall in the middle of your body while driving your knees up to your chest, one at a time, at a ninety-degree angle. Your opposite elbow also reaches up at ninety degrees as you "skip" forward. B skips are essentially an advanced version of As, only with a forty-five-degree extension of your lead leg.

I'm getting bored just describing them.

When I was in high school, we'd do As and Bs for half an hour at a time on some occasions, and I hated it. Even without the rigmarole, I knew I could sprint faster than anyone else, so I didn't see a benefit in the technicalities. Most of my classmates would show up to practice and diligently perform their A and B skips; they'd prepare their bodies all year long by lifting weights and eating right, and yet their fate was always the same: they'd be murdered by me in competition.

I always joke that I'm the Allen Iverson of track and field. *"We in here talking about practice . . . Not a game. We talking about practice. Not a game. Not the game that I go out there and die for and play every game like it's my last. Not the game. We talking about practice, man."*

I assumed I was all but done with track and field. As it turned out, track and field wasn't done with me. To paraphrase my mother, my time just hadn't come.

It was about to.

Bruce Burton was a local coach who ran an independent track and field club called Oakville Legion or Oakville Athletiques. He had kept track of me during high school, and every now and then during my time at Sheridan, he would call to tell me about the upcoming track meets his club was participating in across Ontario. He needed bodies and was always on my case about sprinting the 100- and 200-metre races. I brushed those overtures aside at first, but eventually his persistence caused me to give the competitions at least a cursory thought. I made a small decision that had huge consequences: *What the hell? If I've got a free day from basketball, why not? At least I'd be able to meet some girls at these track events that Bruce is going on about.*

In total, I went to three of the meets and won the 100-metre each time. I thought nothing of it. I would simply arrive, warm up and proceed to leave all my competitors in the dust. Those guys were wholly devoted to sprinting and were trying to claw their way to an eventual spot on the national team. My calling was evident. It was practically reaching out and slapping me across the face. And what did I do? I collected the winner's ribbon or trophy, flashed a smile, posed for some pictures and was gone. I'd wash my hands of track and head straight back to the basketball court.

The distraction of basketball soon resolved itself. My involvement in any sort of organized basketball came to an end when I dropped out of Sheridan following the completion of my first year. School just couldn't hold my attention. Sitting in class and listening to lectures was not my cup of tea. Reading what seemed like endless pages in textbooks didn't excite me. It seemed like a means to an end toward which I was not headed. Don't get it twisted: it's not that I hate books—I've been an avid reader throughout my life—but I gravitate to content that teaches me about my interests.

What did interest me at that point in my life was making money. Since the age of thirteen, I've held some type of job, whether that was working as a counsellor at the YMCA sport camp or delivering food for a local spot named Art's Fish and Chips. I made seventy bucks a night at the latter, tips and wages included, and I was very judicious about saving money. From that first time my father took me to a bank when I was thirteen,

I absorbed everything he taught me about money. For instance, I had a Visa card, and for years I would spend only what I could pay back before interest would apply. I was never charged interest and that resulted in a great credit score. That's solid advice for anyone.

By the time I left Sheridan, I was doing well in a job as a marketing consultant in downtown Toronto. Really, I was a glorified telemarketer, but that was okay by me, as long as the money was good. And it was great.

If you've ever seen the modern-day Martin Scorsese classic *The Wolf of Wall Street*, you'll have an idea of what I was doing. My company didn't own anything; instead, it struck deals with other companies that needed their products sold. We would handle that, doing so by cold calling potential buyers. One day we could be selling stocks; the next we'd be pushing gold. This was the 1980s, and companies were throwing everything at consumers. My colleagues and I would show up to work each morning, receive a quick brief on the day's product along with a call sheet containing phone numbers, then proceed to work the phones. It was straight commission, man, so you ate what you killed. And you can best believe I ate a lot.

I used all of my savings to buy my first home. At age nineteen. Owning a place was a goal that I'd had since my early teenage years. It was ridiculously ambitious, and yet I was determined to gain my independence. The best way for that to happen would be to have a space of my own. I could have my boys over whenever I wanted and never have to worry about using the home phone to talk to my lady friends. Besides those typical teenage reasons, home ownership was all I had ever known. My parents were proud owners of land and real estate in Jamaica, and when I came to Canada, my father had bought his own house. As a young man, I didn't let the thought of renting enter my head. It was own or bust, and I put in the hours to make ownership a reality. I purchased a small townhouse on Litchfield Road that backed onto a ravine. My mortgage was $1,500 a month, and that was eased when one of my former basketball teammates at Sheridan, Garnett, became my roommate and paid half my mortgage as rent.

My father, of course, was not happy that I had dropped out of college. Given he'd raised us with an emphasis on education, I expected no other reaction from him. His own experiences certainly coloured his viewpoint. My dad had only a grade eight education. When his father passed, my dad had had to quit school and help provide for the household. He was the eldest son, and that's just how things were in his time. It was his responsibility to earn money to help support the household and his siblings. Someone abandoning the opportunity for an education seemed foolish to him.

However upset my dad was, he didn't take a hard line on my leaving college. I think he witnessed my lack of interest in academics at Sheridan and felt remorse for his insistence that I go there instead of to one of the U.S. schools that had offered me a scholarship. My decision to pursue work over school was probably the turning point in our relationship, where instead of my father being a dictator of rules, he began to see me as a fellow adult. He came into the city one day to visit me at work, and when he arrived at the office, he told the receptionist, "I'm here to see Donovan."

"Hello," she responded. "Who can I tell Mr. Bailey is here to see him? What's your name?"

My dad was confused for a second, and then became angry. He rarely used swear words, but I'm pretty sure the F-word was on the tip of his tongue.

"No, no. *I'm* Mr. Bailey," he answered. "I'm saying that I'm here to see Donovan, and I believe he works here somewhere."

In the West Indies, there's a hierarchy that exists in male relationships. And that moment at the front desk of my workplace, I believe, went a long way toward changing where I stood in my father's eyes. We never spoke about the encounter he had with the secretary, but sometimes non-verbal communication speaks volumes where the spoken word struggles to make its point. My dad gained an understanding that I was serious about my work. I had left school to cultivate my future, not because I'd quit. I was pursuing goals, like earning money at this job, which led to me purchasing my own house. I imagine that he said to himself, *Oh, well, I certainly prepared my son for life, and he's going to be successful. He's going at his own speed now.*

I had shown him that he could trust in who I was as a person, and so the blow of dropping out of school was softened. Adding to his acceptance was the fact that he and I had talked about his early retirement. The harsh Canadian winters had begun to wear him down, and he wanted to purchase a home in Kingston, where many of his friends had winter homes. He had wisely invested in several properties during his years in Canada, and it was time for him to cash in. His properties had become substantial assets, starting with a small townhouse he had put his money into several years before. Then there was a rental unit, followed by a fourplex on Brant Street in the nearby city of Burlington. My father had been buying, leveraging, renting out, and essentially having other people pay the mortgage on his many properties. Some of the investment properties required fixing up to make them fit for renting out, but as a machinist, my dad was quite handy.

We had a conversation about me buying his amalgamated investments with the help of a vendor take-back, which is essentially a mortgage in which the seller extends a loan to the buyer to secure the sale of the property. It's designed to benefit both parties— in our case, creating generational wealth. My father wanted us to manage that portfolio, as it was important for him to keep the fruits of his hard work inside our family. That freed him up to travel back and forth, while at the same time stabilizing the financial standing of his sons in a way that wasn't possible for most people our age.

So, there I was settling into a comfortable life as I entered my twenties. I bought a Porsche and had some great cash flow coming in from my job and the real-estate portfolio. There was a ladder for me to climb, and my only task was to ascend, step by step. Then, in 1990, I did something no one in their right mind would advise an ambitious young man with his whole life ahead of him to do.

I believe in destiny and that we are put on Earth for a purpose. Some people are lucky enough to find their calling during their youth. For others, it comes much later. In my case, my purpose grabbed me by the collar at age twenty-two and set me on the right path, even though I resisted along the way. To that point, I had taken track and field for granted. I hadn't even raced with Bruce's Oakville Legion team in a while.

One fateful day changed all that.

I have two close friends, Andre Metivier and Hopeton Taylor, who were working out with coach Erwin Turney, pursuing their own callings in track. Andre, a long-jumper, was on scholarship in Ohio at the University of Toledo. He had earned a scholarship with the school. Hopeton had done the same with the University of Minnesota as a triple jumper. They were in town for the summer and had their sights set on making Canada's national team. One of the regional track competitions was going to be held at Etobicoke Centennial Park Stadium, which is just a quick drive up the Queen Elizabeth Way (QEW) from Oakville. I hadn't seen them in a while, and they invited me to come watch. I figured, *What the hell, why not?* It would be nice to hang out with my old pals, and maybe if I went, I'd run into some more old friends.

Centennial Stadium is a small outdoor facility with a capacity of about 2,000 people. It was packed that day and the stands were buzzing. I was sitting among the athletes' families and friends, who filled the long metal benches. The track floor itself was full of competitors. Sprinters and long-distance runners were warming up as track officials raced around keeping everything organized.

I couldn't help but feel the energy in the place. I noticed my heart beating quickly. Adrenalin was coursing through my veins, and as the day went on, I grew intensely excited. I was jumping out of my seat to cheer Andre and Hopeton on during their competitions. Simply being in that environment brought the spirit of competition back to my soul. My body was reacting accordingly. Once their events were over, Andre and Hopeton came over to chat with me and quickly noticed my excitement.

"What's going on?" they asked.

"Nothing. It's all right," I responded.

They could see right through me, though, and persisted. "Do you want to run?" Andre said. "We can lie and say that you belong to a track club. We'll get you some stuff and you run."

That was all it took.

I was wearing a collared shirt, trousers and dress shoes. To give you an idea of how unprepared I was, consider this: I wasn't even wearing underwear. I began to ask around and eventually found a dude who also wore size eleven spikes. I asked him to borrow them, along with some clothes, and he didn't even need to be convinced. He was surprised, but in a good way.

"Oh shoot, you got it like that?" the stranger asked with a smile. "Here you go. Get out there and run."

The encounter seems a lot like destiny when I look back on it. A sympathetic athlete with the right-sized spikes happened to be at the track meet that day. He also happened to be generous and lent a stranger his belongings without expecting anything in return (except his spikes).

I got changed and didn't even have time to warm up before the 100-metre competition. It had been a long time since I'd sprinted with any regularity, about three years, but I wasn't deterred. And it didn't matter in the end. I finished in first place, and it wasn't close. And it wasn't like I was surprised, either. I came in cold and still honestly expected to beat everyone. I had all the bravado and confidence in the world, and the thought of coming in second or worse never entered my head. Andre and Hopeton didn't seem surprised either.

"Oh yeah, we knew you could do it," they said after.

In the fall of that year, both guys reminded me about the up-coming national indoor championships and implored me to at least try to make the Canadian indoor team. I was in, although sprinting still wasn't my number-one priority. I was young and single, and so enjoying myself at the bars and being a bachelor occupied most of my free time. Nonetheless, I was going to at least show up and be ready to compete once the whistle sounded. I just looked at it as adding another element of fun to my life. And that's really all I was interested in at that point.

From my younger days in Jamaica to my high-school tenure in Oakville as a track champ, I knew I could run faster than most people. I've explained that with success pretty much guaran-teed, sprinting wasn't really fulfilling to me. How much true joy can a person derive from looking back at something they didn't need to work as hard as others to accomplish? In the moment, though, competition did provide a sense of satisfaction, and that's important for me to highlight.

As soon as I was placed on the block against other competi-tors, a passion sprung up from deep within. And taking flight in a competition connected me to the same feeling I experienced when I was a child. It was like stepping into a portal that trans-ported me back to Jamaica—a portal that provided me with a feeling of complete mental and physical freedom.

If I sound cavalier about my success, I'll also point out that my entire approach to track and field was rooted in my up-bringing and family dynamic—or so I've come to believe. I knew that no matter what happened in my life, I could always go home. That was like a safety net. Over the course of my career, I realized that many athletes weren't afforded the same luxury. Many sprinters desperately need to be successful, because the impact of failure would be catastrophic to their dependants. It's like a baseball player in the Dominican Republic, for example, whose family won't escape poverty if he doesn't make it to the major leagues. That level of success might be his only way to a better life. I'm fortunate that my parents had made sure there were other futures available to me, and if the worst-case scenario befell me, I could always go back to my marketing gig or even move to Jamaica to live with my mom or dad. I had soft places to land, so to speak. So, compared to some of my competitors, I had nothing to worry about. And less pressure meant less stress. But that doesn't mean I didn't get competitive.

Ahead of the indoor championships, track and field clubs across the country made overtures, trying to convince me to join, as if I were a hot free agent in the NBA. Obviously, it was incredibly flattering, but joining a club was also a practical decision. The clubs arranged transportation to the different meets and handled all the necessary paperwork and fees. I ended up joining the Phoenix Athletics Association in Toronto, a track club close to Oakville that would provide a sort of home base for me. I competed in several meets toward the end of 1990 and the early part of the next year and just kept winning. Winning was enjoyable, of course, but something more intriguing was happening at a few of the competitions: I was besting members of the Canadian national team.

Track and field is as close to a meritocracy as you can get in the sporting world. Whereas in hockey or basketball, players are anointed as "The Next One" at a young age, are awarded prime positions on strong clubs and ultimately get drafted as high picks into the pro leagues, in track, especially sprinting, if you show up and beat the field, nobody's opinion of you matters. You can't be denied. I epitomized that. I had essentially come out of nowhere and quickly began to make a name for myself through my results. Selection to the national team was not determined by anything other than competition times, and soon enough, I was a member. It was an automatic thing, of sorts, with no formality attached. Back then, there was no phone call from a high-level executive welcoming you to the club. You were notified that you might qualify for a stipend, but that was it. I was definitely an outsider, unlike guys in my age group like Bruny Surin and Glenroy Gilbert. That caused at least a few people to wonder, *Who is this guy Donovan?*

I didn't view being on Team Canada as a big deal. Day-to-day life didn't change. Maybe a few more officials would come around to the events, but that was it in the early days. However, I was seeing more media attention at my events. They weren't there for me, though. I was going up against stronger competition, and those sprinters drew a lot more than just local interest.

I loved it. I remember at one point in 1991 running into renowned Canadian broadcaster Rod Black, who showed up to interview Ben Johnson on the occasion of his return from suspension for his failed drug test in Seoul. I walked by the broadcaster and said, "Oh, hey, Rod Black from TV, right? You're here to cover me, right?" He didn't know me at the time and asked who I was.

"Donovan Bailey—remember the name," I said before walking away. I was brimming with an abundance of confidence, and looking back now, I can safely say that my idolization of Muhammad Ali was beginning to manifest in how I carried myself.

CHAPTER 4

WELCOME TO THE DONOVAN SHOW

NO STORY WOULD BE complete without adversity. In my sprinting career, my first bout with something of that nature occurred in 1991. I was humbled on the track for the first time in my life. Hell, I'll keep it 100 percent real with you. It was the first time between the white lines that I was scared.

I was representing Canada at the Pan American Games, which were being held in Havana, Cuba. This was my first dance on such a grand stage since I had been a kid at Champs. Prior to these Games, I had mostly sprinted in regional competitions that received little fanfare. I could go out on the track and do my thing without ever having to think about expectations or the crowd. When I arrived at the brand-new Estadio Panamericano in Havana, I immediately felt a different level of gravitas. The stadium seated over 30,000, and as my name was announced on the sound system ahead of the 100-metre final, I looked up into the sea of spectators and was shook. I had qualified in front of an empty stadium. But now, I was mesmerized by the sheer number of people there for the final and sunk into a dazed state until, suddenly, I heard three words that set me back to reality.

"On your marks."

It was as if I was in a trance. I didn't even hear "Get set." The gun went off.

"Oh my God," I muttered to myself.

This was actually happening. I glanced up and saw all the other sprinters ahead of me. They had left me in their dust, literally. It seemed like I was miles behind them. At that point, my muscle memory kicked in, mixing with the adrenalin, and I began to take flight. However, 100 metres doesn't give you much space to make up for your mistakes. It was too late. I finished in eighth place with a time of 10.76 seconds. I was steaming mad by the time I crossed the finish line. I got down on my knees and pounded the track with my fists. I was more pissed than sad. Very few people had seen me angry till that point, but I let my frustration show. I was upset at myself because I felt that I had screwed up a great opportunity. I'd earned my right to be in this event on this enormous stage, yet I was not prepared for the moment. The athlete who finished in first had done so in a time that I had made handily just a few weeks ago, so it wasn't a question of my ability. It wasn't my body that had lost me this. It was my head.

I knew that the ramifications of this were dire, too. It was going to affect how national team decision makers perceived me. I hadn't come up through the Team Canada system and was something of an unknown commodity to the coaches and staff. My ability to match or even beat the best sprinters in the Canadian system meant the system in which all these people had invested their best efforts had missed something—unless I wasn't as good as my previous results indicated. On the track in Havana, I'd had a chance to prove I was for real in elite international competition and instead caused my doubters to lean into their prejudice against the outsider.

I salvaged my reputation somewhat during those Pan Am Games by anchoring Canada to a silver medal after I'd received the baton in fifth place during the 4x100-metre relay final. However, to me, the damage was done. Lesson learned. I was going to make sure that it never happened again.

The 100-metre sprint track is a perfectly straight line. My journey in sprinting was anything but linear. New challenges awaited me in 1992. For one, I started to collect injuries like they were trading cards. There were bone spurs, hamstring issues and then, most significantly, a torn left quadricep. For the most part, I pushed through the pain. As the competition became tougher, my confidence was becoming a liability. I was treating my body like I was an immature high schooler—I thought I was invincible and could beat all those other guys even though I wasn't in peak shape. I didn't yet appreciate that when pushed to this level, my body—any athlete's body—needed maintenance. That blown quad hit me like a hard slap from reality.

It came at the most inopportune time, too: at the trials to make the Canadian team that would compete at the 1992 Olympics in Barcelona. I won my semi-final and clocked a 10:23, only .02 seconds behind the fastest time. But in that race I tore my left quadricep. Supported by the physio team, I petitioned the selection committee and head coach to excuse me from the final. Running with a blown quad is a bad idea, and I'd established the second fastest time on the team that day anyway. There was no need to prove further that I belonged on the team. It should have been that simple. But as I've seen so many times, Canadian sports bureaucracy never makes it easy. I was told that in order to make the team, I had to run the final.

Even after one year in the national program, I constantly felt like I was running into a massive headwind with team officials. Against the advice of the medical people, I decided to try. We had an hour and a half to get my leg ready. It was swollen and stiff. They massaged it, iced it and stretched it. In the final I lasted 15 metres, but the effort increased the tear, leaving a huge hole in my quadricep that would bother me for years to come (I can feel it to this day). I had to pull up.

I knew immediately that I'd made the injury worse. I was disappointed, and I was angry. My semi-final time was on the board for everyone to see. I had proven what I could do when up against the other Canadian sprinters. But the officials weren't going to cut me any slack, and now I had a serious injury to overcome.

I got to work in rehab, with my sights still set on Spain. If I could race again before the Olympics and post a winning result, the officials could still put me on the team for Barcelona. The pain in my left thigh was the most excruciating pain I had ever experienced, and rehabbing it was mentally draining. I hated it. Take ice baths, for example. That was prescribed to aid in the muscle repair, and like most Caribbean people I absolutely despise the cold. Every single time I dunked my body into that frigid water, I'd unleash a bevy of cuss words. Active release was another dreaded component. A physiotherapist would be jamming their elbow into my leg with the intention of breaking up scar tissue. Take your thumb and push into different areas of one of your calves until you find a tender spot. Then, once you locate it, apply pressure as hard as you can.

It hurts, right? Now, imagine that pain times 100. That's what it took to get me through the injury.

I was able to show fitness ahead of Barcelona, hitting the speed I'd achieved in the semi-final at trials. However, the Team Canada decision makers still opted to leave me off the team—no explanation given. I sat at home in Oakville watching my contemporaries compete in those games, and it stung. I had consistently beaten almost all of those guys in the 100-metre. I had also been left off the world championship track team the previous year, despite posting better times than the athletes selected ahead of me. These decisions from Canadian officials were beginning to add up in my head. I wondered if I was being slighted and worried that my name had been tainted after the mishap in Cuba. That provided me with plenty of fuel, because I had stopped thinking of myself as a guy who just happened to stumble into the periphery of the track and field world. A fire was growing in my belly, and I genuinely felt that I deserved more. I wanted to get back at the bureaucrats for thinking I didn't belong on those teams, and those feelings of resentment didn't fade.

My understanding of what it took to be an elite athlete got a push that winter from an unexpected source. The Canadian bobsled team invited me to Calgary to try out, as they looked a year ahead to the 1994 Winter Olympics in Lillehammer, Norway.

My time at Canada Olympic Park (COP) was the first time that I experienced training in a completely structured environment, where everything was focused on the athletes' drive for success. From the time we woke up and had breakfast, our days were regimented for optimal development and performance, complete with therapy time and daily sessions in the weight room. I had never lifted weights in an organized way, so Calgary was a real eye-opener. My quads were strong, not surprisingly, but my upper body was far behind where it needed to be.

I was feeling great about the training, but getting on the bobsled track was another matter. Even on the dry track, I was scared. A fall at top speed while sprinting can really hurt an athlete, but it was rare. Looking down the winding path of a bobsled track, knowing I'd soon be sliding down it only inches from the surface at well over 100 kilometres an hour? Oh, man. Worse, as a top sprinter, I was trying out as the brakeman, necessarily the fastest guy on the team and the last one into the sled. I crashed a couple of times. It's a difficult position, as after we all get a running start, one by one the team jumps into the sled and tucks in tight for aerodynamics—the brakeman last, when the sled is really starting to move. Jump in, stick my feet wherever

I could fit them, and then rest my helmet on the back of the guy in front of me. It all seemed a little crazy, and for a sprinter accustomed to being alone in his lane, strangely intimate.

Of course, all of this was way worse on the ice track. Plus, it was freezing. But none of this kept me from really appreciating that everything we did at the COP—sleep, breathe, eat, live— was towards the goal of athletic excellence. Even though it soon became clear that I wasn't going to be joining the bobsled team, I stayed in Calgary for nearly six months, working on my damaged quad and training in that healthy environment with an eye to the spring start of track season.

I don't know if the bobsled world is as plagued by politics as track and field, but I was there as a guest, so I was never exposed to anything like that, and it was a peaceful break from track, let me tell you. I had good company in Calgary, too. Sheridon Baptiste was part of that team and a sprinter, too. Glenroy was there, and I stayed with athletes Ken Rose and Stuart Mcmillan after leaving the bobsled program. All remain my good friends to this day.

I was also making a habit of meeting interesting people, without realizing who they were. There was a driver for a European bobsled team, I had no idea which, a balding white guy who struck up a conversation with me. I really enjoyed talking with him, the kind of guy who knows how to connect with people. Some of the other Canadians were surprised to see me chatting with him and asked me later how I knew him. I said I didn't, but he was a cool enough guy, we were just a couple athletes having fun between runs. I didn't know he was Albert Grimaldi, also known as Albert II, Prince of Monaco.

———

As spring approached, it was back to reality. Days ahead of the World Championships in Stuttgart, Germany, I was feeling slighted by my own team—again. I had expected to represent our country in the 100-metre and 200-metre, along with the relay. I qualified for those events, but Mike Murray, a track coach with Team Canada, who was also Robert Esmie's personal coach, told me that wasn't going to be the case. I was told I'd be on the relay squad. His justification was that the guys ahead of me had posted better times. I had a serious problem with that.

Back then, administrators, coaches and athletes could do what I like to call a "create-a-track-meet." They would put together small competitions in random locations like Provo, Utah, or Albuquerque, New Mexico, with little fanfare. The meets weren't advertised, and many times, elite sprinters such as myself weren't invited. So that presented lighter competition against which an athlete could post superior times. The events were engineered to make sure that happened. The clock might stop at just the right moment it needed to for a sprinter, or officials would ignore wind readings that would be deemed illegal in properly monitored races. I never had any of that "help."

The bottom line was that guys who had never beat me head-to-head were all of a sudden beating my times when I wasn't on the track. I found that suspicious, and it coloured my perspective when I was denied the opportunity to compete in Stuttgart. The head coach would have known that none of the guys selected ahead of me could beat me. As for the relay snub, Murray said the team had decided to go with a different quartet. In retrospect, maybe it was the insiders just protecting their turf. But in my eyes, at the time, all of this was purely personal.

On that same day in Stuttgart, at practice, I watched in disbelief as Mike was on his knees, begging sprinters Bruny Surin
and Atlee Mahorn to run the relay for us, and they were weighing their options. They had already competed in their individual
finals. The relay was always run last. I was sitting on the practice
track, thinking this was pathetic. It seemed to me that they were
trying to measure their own small celebrity and whether they
were too big for the relay—and in the meantime, they were holding the entire team hostage. I was pissed. Neither of them was
accomplished enough to take such a position, while I was salivat-
ing to compete. My mind flashed to basketball, of course, and the
scenario was unfathomable to me. I felt like the sixth man dying
for minutes while members of the starting five were staying in
the game longer than they should. Put simply, I didn't think those
guys were big enough to be turning down that opportunity.

I've always worn my heart on my sleeve. People around me
will always know when I'm upset. I can't be fake. So, I didn't
bite my tongue. When I ran into Mike later in the athletes' village, I let him have it. I was proper vexed and cussed the track
coach out accordingly. It was dark outside, and we were standing in the front yard of the residence where I was staying. Athletes passing by heard me shouting and swearing and stopped
to see what was going on. Glenroy Gilbert, my good friend and
training partner at the time, stood nearby with other Canadian
sprinters and observed the action. He was named to the Canadian relay squad, and while he might not have agreed with my
language, he certainly wasn't shocked by my reaction.

After I was done with the coach, I went inside the residence.
I was steaming mad, and when Glenroy, who was my roommate,

joined me, he played the role of good friend and listened to my venting. He stepped aside when he saw me lunge for the table next to us. That's when I rang up the bill for a damaged television. After throwing it against the wall, I made a bold statement to him. It might have seemed outlandish in the moment, but Glenroy didn't bat an eye.

My declaration was simple and prophetic: "When I'm the king here and I run shit, this will never happen!"

It was a pledge that I was never going to allow others to dictate my place again. Place-ism is the word I use; the expectation that I wouldn't overstep the boundaries assumed of me. I had no interest in accepting my place. Untrained and unprepared as I was, all I could see was a team that celebrated mediocrity and participation. I was going to take charge of my own destiny. That outburst changed the trajectory of my career.

In the most positive of ways.

I've mentioned that I admired and wished to emulate the great Michael Jordan, who couldn't be coached effectively by any but the very best coaches in basketball. Who was going to tell him anything about the game he didn't already know, or couldn't figure out how to do even better on his own? His six-time champion Chicago Bulls had coach Phil Jackson. Likewise, my declaration led me to my track and field mentor, a man who changed my life and was largely responsible for fine-tuning me into the world's greatest sprinter.

I had already met Dan Pfaff a few years earlier. He was a short American with a big moustache and dark sunglasses. You could never catch him without a large wad of chewing tobacco in his mouth. Dan looked miserable but turned out to be great company when you dug beneath the layers. And there were plenty of layers to him.

Dan was born in Ohio and, growing up in the 1960s, played whatever sport was in season, from football to ice hockey to wrestling, baseball and basketball. He was a true generalist, and even though he never competed at a high level, Dan grew to become a sought-after track coach. He had been a high-school science teacher after university, and in the 1970s, he spent time touring with U.S. teams in Europe, where he was exposed to the dominant German and Russian athletes. I like to describe him as a savant—he was among the more studious people I have ever met in this industry and knew exactly how to absorb information and then communicate it in an effective way. Some people are *coaches*, while others are *teachers*. Dan was the latter. He empowered you and, as a result, was able to successfully extract every last drop of talent that God gave you. Dan was an expert motivator, but not in the rah-rah cheerleading sense. He trained you up and that allowed him to instill a new and different sense of confidence in you. Every single athlete that he has ever worked with has improved. Every one. That's remarkable for any coach in this world. His technical knowledge led to him becoming a prominent lecturer across the globe, and when I first encountered him in 1991, he was working as an assistant coach on the track team at Louisiana State University.

Dan was Glenroy's coach and took a liking to me when we first met during a relay camp in Baton Rouge. He had been observing me for some time, and while he never said too much, I could tell by the way he spoke during our brief interactions that he was impressed with my abilities. Every now and then, during the camp, Dan walked by me and lobbed a few questions my way: "So how long have you been doing this?" "What was your fall training like?" "Do you run hills?" "What's your base work like?"

I answered no, I didn't do any of that, and he would just nod and walk away. Dan, I was discovering, had a uniquely non-verbal style of communication.

Finally, after we'd spoken a few times, he approached me and said, "Donovan, there are athletes and then there are athletes with a motherf—— in them. A killer instinct. You're that guy. You see red in competition."

Now, this was back in 1991, and as I mentioned, my head was not completely in the game yet. I had never trained full-time or done any of the things he was asking me about, but I was winning regardless. Dan said I should come down to LSU to work with him. I told him I'd join him in thirty days. By the end of the month, that didn't happen. Every week I'd call Dan and give him new excuses: "Hiya, Dan. I'm working on some things. I'll come down soon." Eventually, he stopped taking my calls. It became almost like a joke between us. I think I found it funnier than he did.

Glenroy had told me what life was like training down in Baton Rouge. You could just focus, he said. You were pretty much in the middle of nowhere, so distractions were limited. You spent the entire day training, went back to your room at night, made dinner and hit the bed. A live-to-train-another-day type deal. Dan was a world-class coach and LSU had world-class facilities. The weather was perfect for sprinting, hot and humid.

That all sounded great, but I just wasn't prepared to head down there yet.

Back to 1993 and my heated argument with Team Canada's Mike Murray. Dan, being Glenroy's coach, was around the scene in Germany and heard about what went down. He sought me out, then sat me down and told me I was being disruptive. I guess he must have seen what was left of the television.

I thought highly of Dan and took his words seriously. That made me pause. He was an objective observer in this and really had no agenda other than to coach—and a good coach (which I believed Dan to be) doesn't hold back with the truth. We had a frank conversation, and he reiterated his praise from a few years ago.

Then, he laid into me.

"You're talented. You could be the greatest. You've got to get serious though. You need to hone your skills, train and do this thing properly, because this is clearly not working for you. You compete and get faster every year, but as soon as you gain more speed, you get injured because you have no base. You have no training, and you don't even understand what the hell you're doing. You get out, you put your shoes on and you run. That's it. When you want to get serious, give me a call and come to LSU.

"Anytime you're ready, you can crush everyone."

There used to be a saying about Dan. It went something along the lines of "Dan's going to find the stray dogs and lead them all back to the track." That's exactly what he did with me. After our talk, and still seeing red for having been left off the team again, I felt a sense of urgency unlike anything I'd experienced before. Dan's words had provided a jolt, and I knew what needed to be done.

For the first time in my life, I began to consider that I might be squandering my talents, squandering my purpose. Let me tell you that scared me. I began to put everything in my life in place so that I could go down to Baton Rouge with a clear mind and laser focus.

Firstly, my girlfriend at the time was pregnant with my first child, and I needed to make sure she was taken care of and had everything she needed. I sold my home and tied up the loose ends of my real-estate portfolio. Once I found someone to manage that for me, I had one last item on the checklist—and it was a big one. I had to explain my decision to George Bailey.

I visited my father at his home in Oakville one day in February of 1994 and told him I was leaving my successful business endeavours behind. I was heading to Louisiana to train at track because that was what I wanted out of life.

"Let me get this straight," he said. I don't have to tell you that he was skeptical, to say the least. "At twenty-six years old, you're going to let someone else manage your businesses, you have a baby coming, and you're going to go and run tracks full-time? How much money is that going to pay you, exactly?"

"I think we get a stipend of something like $12,000 to $15,000," I responded.

He was mad as hell. With my real-estate portfolio and burgeoning business interests, including my new restaurant chain Philthy McNasty's, my net worth was in the seven figures, and now I wanted to go run for something like minimum wage. He told me in no uncertain terms that my decision made no sense. To give you an idea of how little regard my father had for track and field in those days, simply observe what he had just said to me and how he'd said it: "You're going to go and run tracks." *Tracks.* Plural. That's how he would pronounce the name of my sport. I explained to him the advantages of becoming a successful full-time sprinter. There were branding, marketing and sponsorship opportunities that could be very lucrative.

"This is the only time I can do it, Dad," I said. "It's the only time. Yes, the baby's coming. That's perfect. To me, it's added pressure on me that makes me more focused. That's always been the case in my life. This is what I'm going to do."

He paused for a minute. The room fell silent, except for the sound of my pounding heart. I didn't know what he was going to say next, and the anticipation was palpable in my body.

"I'm going to support you in whatever it is you do," he said finally. "You know I trust you and believe in you, but I'm not sure that I believe in your timing. And I'm not sure that it's the right time."

"No, no, it's the right time," I said. "I've pinned everything down, and I know everything that's supposed to happen right now, and now I can go away and train mentally free of the stuff that I have going on here."

Betting on yourself is not for the faint of heart. It takes intestinal fortitude. Guts, so to speak. I was looking at a future filled with risk, but the thought of failure didn't even cross my mind. I felt that no matter what happened, I would walk away as a winner. If I went down to LSU and devoted myself to track but didn't improve and my athletic career fizzled out, then that wouldn't be a failure. In my eyes, the act of trying to accomplish something grand, for the right reasons, is a major success in itself. Through that act, you will grow and change and learn valuable knowledge about yourself. Life is enriched by experiences, and this certainly was going to be one.

My father, however, couldn't get past the fact that I was willing to walk away from my business success despite having all these wonderful things going for me so early in life. Such a risk was foreign to him, just as it would be for many working-class West Indians of his generation. He saw the gains I'd made as a reason to be cautious. But I felt I was too young not to strive, especially when my chances of greater success were very real. He stayed upset for a good bit. He didn't talk to me much. When we did interact, it wasn't our usual affable dialogue. It was strained.

Today, I understand the dilemma he was facing. It's the same one that many parents deal with when they move to Canada and raise children. They work so hard and make countless sacrifices so that their children will be set up for success and never have to struggle in the way that they did. And then their kids grow up and risk all the advantage their parents had secured for them through sacrifice. I could understand why my father was angry at me. But I knew what I was doing, and I was going to do it my way.

On the evening of Friday, March 4, 1994, I touched down in Baton Rouge. I called Dan from an apartment where another athlete had agreed to rent me a room, and let the coach know that I was finally putting my money where my mouth was.

"I'm here," I announced.

"You're *here* or you're *here* in Canada?" he shot back.

"No, I'm here," I answered. "It's now or never."

On Saturday I visited him at his office on the LSU campus. Once I got there, we went for a walk around the track. It was a leisurely stroll, but his words had a certain heaviness to them. He told me to forget everything that had happened with Team Canada. He added that it was awesome that I was here, but if I was planning to take any shortcuts, I had come to the wrong place.

Dan is not a person who hugs. At that time in my life, neither was I. But after hearing those words, I had an ear-to-ear grin and instinctively wrapped my arms around him for a big, un-prompted bear hug. We continued around the track, and Dan didn't waste any time diving into business. He stood in front of me for a few seconds and began to analyze my gait. He spat out some of the tobacco in his cheek, paused, then told me that I walked with a strut. Picture a gangster in the movies walking down the street—that's how I walked. It wasn't a conscious thing. That's just how Jamaican guys of my generation walked. There was a dance called "the skank," and it put a swagger in every step of our stride. "I get it," Dan joked. "I know you Jamaican guys and how you're *the man* and all that." I couldn't help but laugh. He knew what was up.

My heels were constantly absorbing the brunt of impact of each step, to the point that I'd even had bone spur surgery a few years prior. You could see the wear and tear on the heels of every pair of shoes I owned. My steps were wildly inefficient, Dan explained, adding that my walking gait, in turn, impacted my running technique. It was like driving a car with one foot on the gas and the other on the brake, he said. I was killing the momentum of each step.

He showed me the correct form, which ensured that the impact of each step was distributed from heels to toes. Dan's intention was to completely break down my sprinting technique and build it up again with optimal form. On that very first day, he even gave me homework. Each morning I had to spend time walking barefoot on the grass and practising the correct heel-to-toe form. Do that every day for the entire year, Dan said, and it would become embedded in my muscle memory, and that would show up in competition. So, I made that walk a habit that I stuck with for the rest of my career. There were many times when I would take my shoes off and walk bare-footed on the track or the infield to monitor how my body felt. Honestly speaking, I probably progressed twentyfold as a sprinter just from that single conversation with my new coach. There was instant, almost innate, synergy between Dan and me. When he showed me how to walk properly, I got it right away, while I know he still had to explain the importance of being light on your feet to some other athletes who'd been under his watch for years.

On Monday, I showed up to my first practice and was exposed to more of Dan's unique style of teaching. Outside of my time in Calgary, I had never seriously lifted weights, a fact that would strike today's athletes as absurd. My maximum bench press at that time would probably have been 120 pounds. For context, my pal Glenroy was likely pushing 300 pounds. I needed to improve.

Dan walked over to the area where the female athletes were training and introduced me to Laverne Eve, an extremely strong Bahamian Olympian who threw the javelin. "This is Donovan. He's never lifted weights before," he said.

I was overcome with embarrassment and looked at it in the same way any young Caribbean man from that time would: Dan was challenging my manhood. He doubled down and arranged for me to lift along with the women. I simply could not keep up. They would load up the leg press with a pile of plates, and I could barely move it. Yet here they were pushing the cast iron with complete ease, barely breaking a sweat with twice the weight I was lifting.

Of course, my ego was bruised and I was pissed. However, the entire ordeal served to accomplish Dan's intended purpose, which was to stoke the fire in me and make me realize the need to get to work. He needed to get me interested in lifting, and this was his way of doing so. I was surprised to learn that weight training is paramount to a sprinter's success. When someone is in full speed on the track, the torque that moves through their muscles is ten to twenty times more than their body weight. So, it's vitally important to make sure that each muscle and every tendon is strong enough to withstand that.

I was determined to change my body and grew obsessed with getting stronger. I was churning out hundreds of push-ups every day in my rental room, adding the exercise to my morning routine of walking barefoot. I also sought to lift anything I could get my hands on—chairs, luggage bags, an ottoman. I didn't have a barbell at home, so I practised bodyweight squats and clean and jerks in front of the mirror with a keen eye on perfecting my form.

Weight training for any professional athlete is wasted unless accompanied by a strong dietary regimen. As you could have guessed, my nutrition was poor when I arrived in Baton Rouge. I was accustomed to living the party lifestyle, hitting restaurants and then nightclubs. Dan quickly turned that around. He got me taking vitamins, eating and hydrating properly and increased my healthy carbohydrate intake. Instead of white bread, which I could buy for ninety-nine cents per loaf in those days, I adopted whole wheat bread. The same went for white rice versus the brown version, which is packed with more fibre, magnesium and other nutrients. At least I could still eat my beloved Jamaican staple of rice and peas.

The amount of protein I consumed shot up, too—the *right* protein. Dan asked me one day if I ate pork. "Of course," I responded. "I'm Jamaican." He remarked that, according to his research, pork could weaken an athlete's tendons. That was all I needed to hear. I dropped pig from my diet immediately and didn't resume eating it until much later in life, well after my retirement. Instead, I was eating chicken breasts or drinking protein shakes every couple of hours. I made frequent visits to a grocery store called Kroger, which was kind of like what Whole Foods is now. After a quick stop there, my fridge was stocked with fresh fruit and cooked rotisserie chicken. I didn't have to put too much thought into grocery shopping, a fact that I appreciated. A wonderful aspect about life in America is the incredible all-you-can-eat restaurants. Back in those days, you could hit up a breakfast spot and eat until your stomach was content for about three bucks. I was going through the buffet and loading up my plate with only the healthy options, such as omelettes and veggies.

Dan also taught me that water is crucial. I had never been a fan of drinking water, as silly as that sounds. Believe me, plenty of people in my life laughed when I told them that. I just didn't like the empty taste. I'd want flavoured water or juice, which would at least arouse my taste buds. I came to understand, though, that I was not adequately replenishing the fluids lost during competition, and that was playing a major role in my chronic injuries. Who would have thought that drinking water would have provided such a eureka moment? The weather was scorching when I was down in Baton Rouge. It was 100 degrees Fahrenheit every day, with thick humidity that would consume you. In that kind of weather, I was soon bringing a giant jug of water to LSU every day, without a reminder.

Dan also enlightened me on how ten hours of sleep could rejuvenate my body and help it recover. Suddenly, I couldn't wait to hit the pillow at night. That was something the previous version of myself would never have imagined. The twenty-one-year-old version of me getting to bed early? Forget that.

These changes worked wonders. I'm addicted to success, and so the goal-setting aspect of my training at LSU kept me driven. For example, if Dan gave me a weight to hit on the leg press, I'd make sure I got there quickly. If he wanted me to get eight hours of sleep each night, I'd forego all kinds of late-night distractions that stood in my way. My body was clearly changing—I left Canada weighing about 170 pounds and put on about 15 pounds of muscle in two months. It was well distributed across my body. My shoulders, chest and quadriceps were bigger, and my traps looked like they were popping out. I was strong as hell. And I took pride in going about my business the natural way.

I was enjoying myself, too. At the track, I'd put on my head-phones, pop in a mixtape and work through my warm-up routine, skipping around the track with my mind elsewhere until I was ready to sprint. I made a friend while running indoors in 1992 named Yvette Blackburn. She was competing for the University of Windsor, and she was a huge dance hall fan. We stayed in touch, and whenever I needed something new to listen to, she'd put out a call to the DJ groups she knew—Stone Love, King Turbo, Killamanjaro, others—so there was always something fresh in my headphones, someone on the turntable, someone on the mic, someone rapping. I'd get those tapes, usually live recordings cut into mixes, and my daily routines went a lot faster. To this day, music is my happy place. I fly friends to Jamaica for Reggae Sunsplash, Rebel Salute, Sting, all the big festivals. But I'm losing myself in music now, because there were serious matters at the track other than our training, and they're a lot less fun to think about.

Performance-enhancing drugs (PEDs) were seared into the track and field conversation in the late 1980s by Canadian sprinter Ben Johnson. He won gold in the 100-metre dash at the 1988 Olympics in Seoul, only to have the medal stripped from him when he tested positive for steroids. I'll get into his story a little later, but the context matters. His transgressions cast a long shadow on every sprinter that followed, particularly Canadians. PEDs were around when I competed, but there was no chance in hell I would ever take that route. In fact, I drove myself nearly crazy in my attempts to avoid them. When I was training at LSU in 1994, for example, there were times when I'd go out to eat with other athletes. We loved this Cajun-style seafood place, and I would order my food and water and stay in my seat until every last morsel and drop were consumed. I never got up and left my plate or glass unattended, not even for a washroom break. When I was practising around other athletes on the track, I kept my knapsack away from the rest and always in a spot where I could easily see it. When I went to nightclubs during the off-season, later in my career, I never ordered mixed drinks. I'd only get bottles of beer or liquor and ask that it be opened in front of me. That was the level of discomfort I had around strangers, and I never wanted to be in a situation where I ingested something accidentally. Nobody cares about "accidents." I've heard athletes' excuses about taking the wrong vitamins, for instance, but that doesn't fly with me. The bottom line is that a banned substance was found in *your* body. That's on *you*, as the athlete. With the level I could perform at even before I started training with Dan, I now saw myself becoming a brand and an ambassador for track and field, and if I tested positive for anything, just once, it would ruin everything. There were no false starts when it came to PEDs.

I competed in the late 1990s against American sprinter Maurice Greene, and while he never failed a drug test during his career, his name was linked to a doping scandal. He was one of twelve athletes named—including jailed former Olympic champion Marion Jones, who confessed to using PEDs though she had never failed a drug test—who were reportedly supplied with the drugs by a former discus thrower from Mexico. Greene called the situation "embarrassing." He said that while he did know the discus thrower, Ángel Guillermo Heredia Hernández, he never took PEDs himself. The discovery of a U.S.$40,000 cheque Greene had written to Hernández was the first time that Greene's name had been publicly linked to drug use, but it takes only one report for PEDs to be connected to your name forever. Even if you didn't do it, the whispers would still be enough to drown out your good reputation.

*

Dan augmented my change in body composition with a warm-up routine that was unlike anything I had done before. He had me doing dynamic stretches for close to two hours before any strenuous physical activity or training. The idea was to activate every single muscle I could. He called it "stimulating the nervous system," which would allow me to get the most out of every single workout.

Oh, and remember A and B skips? Dan had once described my motions as "uncoordinated" and "awkward," but now my skips were the picture of perfect form. I embraced plyometric training and learned to master what Dan called "basic sport literacy menu items," like skipping for height and distance, scissor bounds and hopping over hurdles.

When it came time to put everything together on the track, Dan introduced me to an interesting mental trick to simplify the execution of a 100-metre competition. The race could be broken into three segments:

1. **Acceleration:** This phase is the start of the competition, which is the area I always struggled with. Part of that was likely due to muscle misalignment along my spine, which

hindered my ability to explode in a straight line off the blocks. According to Dan, a combination of my injury history, genetics and mental focus put a ceiling on my starting ability, and it was something we needed to constantly be aware of and work on. Expressing dominant power on your first few steps is critical, and ideally, you want to launch out of the blocks into peak acceleration as quickly as possible—within the first twenty metres— before moving to the next step.

2. **Float and Sprint:** In general, most athletes will hit their top speed somewhere around the fifty-metre mark. Once you achieve that speed, you're actually in the air more than your feet are touching the ground. Look at any photo of a sprinter in the middle of the 100-metre. Usually, their feet are well above the track, as if the athlete were in flight. Think of it as a "floating" state.

3. **Relaxation:** The last thirty metres of the competition might seem a little paradoxical. Dan wanted his runners to breathe and relax while operating at maximum veloc- ity. In this final stretch, you are at your most powerful stage. You've hit your genetic potential and literally can't go any faster. You can only lose speed from here to the finish line. The key, therefore, is to minimize how much speed you lose. You want to lose that speed *slower* than your competition loses theirs. Dan called it "decay." "Reduce the amount of decay you have in your speed," he said to me. To do that, I learned to calm my breathing

and body to help me keep my optimal mechanics and efficiency intact. Don't deviate because you see the finish line approaching, he instructed. Sprinters have a tendency to decelerate and then leap forward as they touch the line. That costs time in the end, which is, of course, what Dan wanted to avoid. A sprinter's mettle is really tested in the final stretch of a sprint, and that's what Dan got me to understand. The body is inclined to tense up in those final metres—mine certainly did, and it would result in my shoulders creeping up higher and higher. We worked on being cognizant of that slight change and keeping my shoulders in place while I was in motion.

Ever since I was a child, I had sprinted with reckless abandon. My coach, however, harnessed that chaotic form into a more precise and powerful weapon on the track. As you can probably tell, I have all the respect in the world for Dan. It wasn't just what he taught me, but *how* he taught me. He provided structure, a personalized version of what I'd had a taste of in Calgary. I was his "project," just like I was with Wayne Allison, my Sheridan basketball coach, years ago.

Though they were very different men in many ways, Dan reminded me of my father. I had the utmost confidence in both men and their words. From the time I was a little boy, I have implicitly trusted my father. He always had my best interests in mind, and I knew he would do anything for his children. With Dan, I got that same feeling—he would do anything for his pupils. He had children of his own, but I could see in his body language that he hurt like hell when his athletes didn't do well.

He'd drop his head, just a little, take the tobacco out of his mouth and toss it aside, and go for a short walk. There were so many people under his watch aside from myself and Glenroy—we're talking in the hundreds here. And while he was responsible for bringing many medals to Canada, Dan trained people of all nationalities. Our training sessions included athletes from Germany, Finland and Mexico, to name just a few of the countries they'd come from.

When the U.S. Track & Field and Cross Country Coaches Association inducted him into its Coaches Hall of Fame in 2018, the organization listed his contributions as guiding thirty-three athletes (ten medals) to the Olympic Games. Five athletes he coached set world records under his direction. Additionally, he's lectured in a whopping thirty-seven countries and been published in more than twenty.

Much of that hadn't happened by the time I moved to Baton Rouge, but Dan quickly won my respect anyway. He was an athlete's coach. He spent time trackside with all his athletes or on the phone explaining in detail why he was directing them to do the things he was. I was taught to place value on my time and energy, and Dan never wasted either. He never left me wondering why I was trying to make a particular change in my gait or starting position or anything else. And man, his thought processes and philosophies were deep. He showed me articles he had written about training strategies. He studied the benefits of Eastern medicine and spent hours educating me on the science behind acupuncture, massages and hot and cold treatment. I trusted him, and when an athlete trusts a coach who has that much to offer, that dynamic serves as the foundation for success.

He once told me something I'll never forget: "Your human machine is the greatest thing on Earth, and what we can do is train it in order for it to maximize its entire strength in every single way. We can do this to be ready to compete on Saturday or six months from now. The choice is yours." It was one of those strings of words that penetrate your consciousness and spark something deep inside of you.

Dan was very different from my father in one respect: George Bailey told his sons what to do. It was understood that we were going to do whatever he said, like the time he told me to stay in Oakville for school instead of going to the States—and that was fine. My brothers and I were raised in an environment where Father knows best, and we weren't going to question him or talk back. Dan didn't dictate; he communicated. Dan would tell me, "Here's what I want you to do. I need you to get this done by this day." After that request, though, he would continue to check in with me to gauge my thoughts and feelings: "Do you feel lighter? Do you feel heavy? Do you feel flat-footed?" We had constructive dialogue and feedback, which was important to me, because I'm naturally inquisitive, forever the "why kid." And he'd take the time to engage in conversations even while simultaneously working with a dozen other athletes. It felt like I was learning something new each day in Louisiana. For that, I'll forever be grateful.

During my time at LSU, I was renting a room in a townhouse that belonged to a long-jumper named Dennis. It was in the rough side of town, and I was paying him U.S.$90 a month. It wasn't a great living space—the mattress seemed like it was made in the 1800s—but I made do. I could get used to the accommodations, but I never did get used to Dennis. I remember one night, after I'd wrapped up with Dan and had something to eat, I got back to the townhouse and saw Dennis with a bunch of friends sitting by the dinner table. I nodded to them as I walked by and heard Dennis mutter to his pals, "Oh yeah, that's the Canadian guy. He's staying in the scrub room." I thought, *Who the fuck is this guy?* However, I stayed civil, collected receipts for later accounting and kept moving. I wasn't going to waste my energy getting into a fight with Dennis. Maybe a few years earlier I would have entertained the drama, but not now. I was on a mission.

I eventually did manage to get back at him. I was at LSU exactly one year later for the shooting of a Powerade commercial. At this point I was the reigning world champion and the number-one ranked sprinter on the planet. It was 100 degrees Fahrenheit that day, and there were stand-ins, or body doubles, who were hired to stay outside in the blazing Louisiana sun in place of the main talent for less crucial aspects of the filming process. Dennis was one of them. I was in my trailer when I suddenly spotted Dennis outside. He was walking toward my trailer and was promptly stopped by a security guard who told him that he wasn't allowed in this area; it was reserved for main talent only. Later on, when it was time for me to head to the track for my segment of the shoot, I ran into Dennis, of course. I walked by him, smiled and said, "Yeah, you're in the scrub room now."

Accounts settled.

———

Twelve weeks after I had landed in Louisiana, I felt it was time to see some competition. Track season was underway, and I was burning to try out my new game. I told Dan, and he raised his eyebrows. He didn't think I was there yet, but I was headstrong and he said okay. I found an agent in Germany, got in contact and before long he had booked me a flight overseas for an event. He didn't purchase a first-class seat, and I made the trip at the back of the plane. Sprinters' thighs and coach seating aren't a comfortable combination. Sitting with my legs squeezed together wasn't the ideal scenario for me if I was going to be competing soon after arrival in Germany. The plan was to hit the road with a few of his other clients, sharing hotel rooms and competing at regional events.

In Cologne, I took a cab to the agent's house. We had never met before. There was no internet or social media back then to check somebody out, and I had been referred to him by someone else. The agent's name was Walter, and he was nice enough. He offered to let me sleep at his place and recover from the long, cramped flight. He was preparing to drive for an hour to a track meet in Rellingen, where some other athletes he was representing were going to compete, and he offered to let me tag along if I felt up to it. I could use the opportunity to warm up, work the jet lag out of my legs and get a look at the competitors. Of course, I was raring to go, despite the stiff legs and jet lag.

I brought my spikes and shorts with me, and once we arrived at the meet, I began to warm up my body and work away some of the stiffness. I had no intention of competing, but as I limbered up, my feelings changed. There was a sprinter from Ghana there by the name of Emmanuel Tuffour. He was considered the "fast guy" at the meet, and of course, hearing someone mention that immediately stoked my competitive fire.

As I went through the motions and chatted with other sprinters, my competitive instinct was tingling. I found Walter and told him that I wanted in. He was taken aback and tried to persuade me against it. "You just came off the plane this morning. I don't want you to get injured." I told him not to worry, that I felt good and knew what I was doing.

I continued my warm-up with more concentration, using the precise routine that Dan had taught me. I buckled down for about ninety minutes and methodically activated all of my muscles until it was go time. I ended up sprinting 10.50 in my heat, fast enough to win it. Emmanuel ran in a separate heat and was a tick faster, setting a meet record of 10.46. We had both advanced, and there was a short break before we were set to go head-to-head in the final.

Walter was Emmanuel's agent as well, and I remember Emmanuel walking up to him during the break with a demand. He asked Walter to go and collect his appearance fee and his bonus for setting the meet record. We hadn't even run the final yet, and Emmanuel was acting like he had already won.

Now, I'm sure he didn't mean any disrespect to me by making his demands on Walter. Emmanuel was a pretty cool dude. Nevertheless, I was seeing red. I didn't let it show, but I was thinking that this guy had no idea who he was dealing with. We hadn't even faced off yet and he thought it was over.

I didn't need the extra motivation. Given my training in Louisiana, I was primed and ready to win. But it didn't hurt to have that fuel thrown on the fire. When the event began, I was given lane four, which I was pleased with. The most favourable lanes for the 100-metre are four, five and six. You will rarely find a world or Olympic champion winning from lane one or lane nine. If you're in either of those spots, you're kind of like a man on an island. There's only one person beside you, while the other side is empty. The other competitors are far away. I always looked at the middle lanes as a vortex in which you can feel the energy of the other sprinters. You're not looking at them— you've got your proverbial blinders on—however, you can certainly *feel* them. Sensing their energy fueled my adrenalin. You're right in the middle of the action, and so your body has no choice but to show up and show out.

I certainly showed out against Emmanuel. I had ramped up my acceleration with Dan and it worked; I came off the blocks quickly. Not only could Emmanuel not touch me, but I also crushed the meet record that he had just set.

As I sauntered off the track, I looked Emmanuel in the eye. Then I looked at Walter and made my own demand: "Walter, how much money do I owe you for the flight? Okay, good. Go collect that and take it out of my sum along with your percentage. I want my money and my bonus, and next time I want my own hotel room!"

Emmanuel heard every word I'd said.

I won my first professional trophy that day, a bottle of wine. I still have it, though I'm sure it's undrinkable by now.

I continued to compete across Europe that summer, still with only very limited training from Dan. It didn't slow me down. I signed my first professional contract that season with Fenerbahçe

Athletics in Türkiye. For a month, I stayed in a nice hotel in Istanbul and represented the team in the European club championships.

Turkish cuisine reminded me of Jamaican food, and the weather was fantastic. A coach and some of the athletes spoke broken English, enough that I didn't struggle to communicate. I was there only a month, but I enjoyed it. The other sprinters weren't very athletic, but they'd give their left arm to win in competition, and I appreciated their desire to win.

At one of my first practices, I noticed one of them taking a cigarette break.

"Dude, you're smoking?!" I said. In the '90s, you might have caught North Americans in team sports still sneaking a cigarette, but a sprinter? No way.

"I smoke, I smoke," he replied with a shrug.

I just shook my head and laughed. "Okay."

As the others got to know me, they'd watch me train for the relay and say, "There he is! That's our guy!" I'd be thinking, "What do you mean, I'm your guy? Hey, you've got to run a leg too!"

Before the month was through, I'd anchored the 4x100 relay team to a new national record.

The wins piled up that year, and with no shortage of confidence I could say that I was now the number-one sprinter in Canada. Bruny Surin had set the Canadian 100-metre record of 10.02 seconds in 1993—that record was my only competition, not the other sprinters. I was getting close in my races, hitting 10.07, then 10.05. I knew that the record would be mine eventually. It was me against the record books.

In June of 1994, I sprinted against Glenroy and Bruny at a meet in Duisburg, Germany. This was the first time since I'd started training with Dan that we lined up in competition, and it was also the first time I met American 200-metre champion Michael Johnson. I ran and won my semi-final. Michael dropped into the final, which an established star could do at a professional meet without running the qualifying heat. In the finals of the meet, the winners of the two semis are given the centre lanes. Michael wanted the lane that was assigned to me, so I was bumped one over. I still had a good lane, but I wasn't going to take getting moved around by anyone. I thought to myself, *This guy has no idea what's about to happen.*

The gun went off and I had a great start. I was ahead at the thirty-metre mark. At the eighty-metre mark, I had already built up enough of a lead that I decided to shut it down. The race was mine and everyone knew it, so I decelerated and looked around at the audience. I finished at 10.03 and could have broken the Canadian record then and there but the win would do for now; I wanted to prove a point and send a message.

When we passed the finish line and were collecting ourselves, Glenroy came up to me and grabbed me by the arm. "Bruny is swearing in French again," he said with a smile. "Tabernacle!" I didn't know what that meant, but with that win I knew I had arrived. I'd shut it down at 80 metres and still finished one hundredth of a second off the Canadian record.

This was precisely what I had been working toward. When I took umbrage with Team Canada the previous year and made my proclamation about being king, this is what I'd envisioned.

It was my "Welcome to the Donovan Show."

The event wasn't televised, so I called Dan afterwards to let him know my time and, more importantly, how I felt during the competition. It didn't matter to Dan who I had defeated. That's one thing about our conversations: they never focused on other sprinters. He didn't care about the noise and taught me to think with that mindset.

He used to say, "You are going to crush them; it doesn't matter who it is." Dan's unwavering confidence was another thing that reminded me of my father. When I was younger and having a conversation with my dad, I might mention someone I was competing with, and he would stop me and say, "No, you're smarter than them," or "You're better than them." While that might not always have been true, when you hear people in your corner pumping you up like that, it breeds a distinct level of self-confidence, and that was integral to my success.

Dan coached his athletes for free. He was paid by the university to coach students, and he coached professionals like me on the side. That didn't sit well with me. By 1994, I was top-five in the world, and I'd just signed a multi-million-dollar sponsorship contract with Adidas (whose other recent signings included Boris Becker, Zinedine Zidane and Steffi Graff). And yet my coach had mentioned to me that he'd never even owned a house. I was getting so much from his teaching and earning money at meets all over the world. I was shocked. I told him I'd owned my first house at the age of nineteen.

I was going to make sure that my track coach who had never owned a house at least owned a great track suit. I asked for a nice one in his size from Adidas and presented it to him. He was thankful, in his understated way. When he got home he noticed the packaging had already been opened. He looked inside and found a few stacks inside. My coach would now be able to put down a deposit on a house.

The next day at the track he smiled and said to me, "Nicest track suit I ever had. It's going to go a long way."

Nothing more needed to be said.

By this point, 1994, I had worked out a lot of the kinks in my game and was beginning to achieve a different level of comfort on the track and within the track and field world. I was 100 percent healthy and had no lingering injury concerns. My body was like a brand-new Porsche, fresh off the lot. I was following what Dan had taught me about warm-ups and execution, and I was acclimating to travel, press conferences and dealing with the media. Things were really coming together, priming me for what was to come. However, there was still more to learn. And that was always my mindset—there were only two possible results in anything I did: win or learn.

About a month after my victory in Duisburg, there was a competition in Rome called the Golden Gala. All the top sprinters in the world were there—Americans Carl Lewis and Leroy Burrell, as well as Linford Christie of Great Britain and Frankie Fredericks of Namibia. I was in there, too. Don't let that chip on my shoulder fool you; I was honoured to be mentioned in the same breath as that group of superior athletes.

I got out of the blocks well in that competition and felt that I was in the lead around the eighty-metre mark. But my brash confidence got the best of me. I took my eye off the finish line and glanced over to see where the other guys were. I couldn't help myself. And I paid the price. I finished in third place.

That one turn of the head can make quite the difference to a sprinter. In order to compete at the highest level, every single facet of your mechanics has to be in line. That slight turn of my head caused my shoulder to drop, which in turn lowered my diaphragm. When that occurs, it means that your leg can't lift high enough to cycle through its optimal range of motion. That's from just taking a quick peek over your shoulder.

As I watched Carl Lewis celebrate, I had the same feeling of sickness in my stomach that I had felt years before in Havana. I kneeled on the ground and laid both hands on the track. I looked up at the stadium's big screen to watch the replay and couldn't believe my eyes. I thought, *Oh my God, I was racing against the greatest sprinters in the world. I was ahead of them and I screwed up.*

I was incredibly angry with myself and vowed that it would never happen again. I'd had a level of killer instinct in me before that day, or as Dan had put it, a "motherf——." But going forward, I would make sure that my sword was even sharper. Juxtaposed to my anger, though, was a feeling of happiness. I guess it was the instant realization that I had just had an experience that would lead me to correct my path, almost like the lane-centring feature of a car. I think I even started smiling. I hadn't suffered a loss in the competition: I'd learned what I needed to do to win. I had taken my foot off the gas pedal in Germany and still won. This time I took my foot off the gas pedal and crashed.

Noted.

I could always rely on my confidence to pick me up. I told myself, *You got third place, but that's okay, because the two athletes who finished ahead of you—Lewis and Fredericks—are two of the top sprinters in the world today, and now you know you can beat them.*

Two other major competitions that summer had a profound effect on me. First up was the Francophone Games, held that year in July in Paris. I knew those games were more important to Bruny than most, him being a francophone from Quebec. He was deadly serious around the track on the day of the final. Something about that brought out the antagonist in me. The 100-metre guys are always trying to get under each other's skin and mess with their opponents' heads.

There was always talk around Athletics Canada that Bruny and I were rivals. We weren't. When I finally hit my stride as a global competitor, he was Canada's next fastest sprinter. But there were probably a dozen international competitors consistently closer to what I could do on the track and what Bruny could. When I thought of the competitors who might have qualified as my rivals, he wasn't one of them. But, maybe in Athletics Canada's eyes, I was the outsider, while Bruny was the guy who had been groomed and supported for years by a national system that was layered with executives, coaches, agents and more. They had invested in him, made him their favourite son. And I was a guy with a dominant personality, who showed up to the party late and uninvited, kicked in the door and started destroying competitions and the record books. I was a leader who had no problem calling people out on their shit. I carried myself with a different degree of swagger and had a more bold, in-your-face manner of speaking. Some people in charge didn't appreciate that. They would have liked to think their best guy was good enough to be my rival. He wasn't.

"I'm going to give this one to Bruny," I said, making sure he was near enough to hear me. I was chiding him, but I was also serious. There are times when you need a top finish, and there are times when you just want your opponents to know you're able to beat them. This was the latter, though I wasn't immune to Bruny's deep desire to show well at those games. To all the athletes on the Quebec and New Brunswick teams, the games meant a lot. Also, with only twelve weeks of training in Louisiana, my body wasn't well prepared for the rigours of a whole track season. Dan cautioned me to be careful.

Bruny didn't say anything. He was so dialed in that day. I was good to my word and shut it down at 65 metres. He took home the gold with a 10.08, and I finished second with 10.27.

Maybe I should have beaten him anyway.

A month later, the Commonwealth Games were being held on home soil, in Victoria, British Columbia. I had that event circled on my calendar. I wanted to break the world record on Canadian soil, an event that would introduce me to *everyone* in my country, not just track fans. I was robbed of that coming out party, though, when Canadian officials passed me over to select Bruny—who was coming off surgery—to compete in the 100-metre event. I had a fever of 108 during trials and was advised by the doctors I didn't need to compete to make the team in Victoria. I was number-one anyway. I would have competed, if I'd thought it was necessary, but was advised to rest. So now I was shocked. I'd been beating Bruny routinely by a tenth of a second. Except in Paris.

In Victoria, I crossed paths with Linford Christie in the athletes' village. He laughed out loud with astonishment when I told him he wouldn't be seeing me in the 100-metre final. Hearing his disbelief at the Canadian decision ratcheted up my fury. Linford was one of the best 100-metre sprinters in the world, already a world champion and the reigning Olympic champion from Barcelona. And he was relieved not to face me. To this day, I am frustrated by the stupidity of the Canadian selection committee's decision.

Venting to the media was one way to handle my anger, but once you put your complaints out there, you can't take them back. When it came to my frustration with Canadian track officials, I had one sympathetic ear who really understood what it meant to be stuck in the Canadian system. One of our coaches was a former athlete named Molly Killingbeck. Born in Jamaica, Molly moved to Canada at a young age and became a successful 400-metre athlete. She represented the country in various international competitions in the 1980s, highlighted by her Olympic appearance in 1984, when she captured the silver medal in the 4x400-metre relay. We had become friends in the 1990s, when she was a volunteer with Athletics Canada and a sprint coach at the University of Windsor. I could relate to her in so many ways, and a mutual respect existed between us. Molly had competed at the highest level and was familiar with dealing with the media and, more importantly, navigating the politics within the Canadian track and field landscape. As well, back then, there were few other Black coaches in the Canadian system, and that fostered an unspoken bond between us.

Molly was a voice of reason I sometimes needed to hear and a confidante. Anytime I needed an ear, she was there to hear me out. I could call her up and trust that what I said wasn't going to be repeated. She had been through the system herself and was now seeing it from the inside, which was helpful. She knew officials still saw us as amateur athletes, and they were getting in my way. I saw myself as a professional building a globally recognizable brand, and they saw athletes as property they controlled and positioned as they saw fit. The business model I had in mind was professional sports, whereas the people in charge of Athletics Canada just figured there's a future Olympian born every day—we were lucky to be there and should be grateful for the opportunity.

Not me.

After learning I'd been left out of the 100-metre, I was heated when I picked up the phone to dial Molly's number. She heard what I had to say—and I had a lot to say. As she always did, Molly came back at me with a heaping dose of wisdom. What she said boiled down to this: the best way to get my revenge was to continue to win.

"Don't get angry," she said. "If you keep showing up and doing what you're supposed to do, then you know that the performance will speak for itself." At the end of the day, if I continued to show up, continued to perform and cross the finish line first, then there would be no debate. She reminded me that in most cases in track and field, you're selected based on performance. The 1994 Commonwealth Games were an anomaly in that subjectivity on the part of officials was involved. But this was rare. Because it kept happening to me, though, it didn't feel rare.

Instead of focusing on the slight, I shifted my mindset to a place of pride. Many fans were at the Commonwealth Games to see me. So I decided to give our fans a reason to jump out of their seats and go ballistic during the relay event. I was the leadoff runner, responsible for establishing a strong start for my teammates. And that's exactly what I did. I had told my teammates I was going to give them a fifteen-metre lead to begin the competition. I had wanted to break the world record here and win two golds, so if the relay team wasn't committed to making sure I went home with at least one gold medal, we were going to have a serious problem between us. Carlton Chambers had just come from the NCAA (National Collegiate Athletics Association) championship and Bruny was freshly back from an injury, but I didn't care. I had come here to have my moment, and one chance to do that had been taken away from me. I was going to make it happen with the one chance I had left. I followed through, blazing out of the starting blocks. I handed the baton off to Glenroy, who was the backbone of our relay team. Before the race, I had told him I was going to give him a ten-to-fifteen-metre lead. Which I did. I could always trust him. He was like clockwork in a relay, and he wasn't ever going to mess up. Once he had the baton in his hand, the race was effectively over.

We captured the gold and set a Commonwealth Games record time in the heat and then broke it in the finals with a time of 38.39 seconds.

After the Commonwealth Games, my frustrations led me to confront a question that was threatening to radically change my career trajectory. I had signed that multiyear endorsement deal with Adidas. True to my intentions, I was a professional athlete. And like any professional at the top of their game, I was going to determine my own future.

I met with representatives from the International Olympic Committee (IOC) and International Amateur Athletics Foundation (IAFF). I had competed earlier that year in Türkiye, and because I was a naturalized Jamaican citizen, Türkiye and other countries were reaching out to ask if I'd like to race for their national teams, including the UK and Jamaica. Make no mistake, I wanted first and foremost to compete for Canada, but my own country was burying me beneath inferior athletes and politics.

At the meetings a detail of the international rules became clear: I would have to sit for a two-year cycle of competition before resuming competition under a different flag. That would mean missing the world championships and Olympics, and the only way around the penalty would have been if Athletics Canada signed off on the transfer. They said they would never do that.

As ever, Molly had sage advice. I had extraordinary momentum, and it would be detrimental to my career if I disappeared from international competition right now. I should stay and work on my game. Athletics Canada and the COC (Canadian Olympic Committee) would have to come around, so long as I kept winning.

So, I had no leverage against the Canadian team—unless I made it so clear to the whole world that even the biggest Donovan Bailey detractors would be forced to admit it: Canada's only hope of a 1995 world championship was me. I was top-five in the world, and we had no one else in the top ten. Put me in, and I'd be number one.

So that fall I signed on to compete in the winter indoor circuit. I was going to rack up a slate of wins that would make a profound statement going into 1995. I wasn't much interested in indoor competition, but I had a goal. And when I have a goal, I don't stop until I achieve it.

That winter, I attracted further interest from an unexpected source: NFL teams were calling to ask if I wanted to play football. The expansion teams the Jacksonville Jaguars and Carolina Panthers came knocking, as did the Atlanta Falcons and Oakland Raiders. Oakland expressed interest in drafting me, but I told them I didn't want to play football. The BC Lions of the Canadian Football League drafted me anyway. I did some test runs at LSU, clearing the standard forty-yard dash in between 3.78 and 3.80 seconds. A serious NFL wide receiver can sprint that distance in as low as 4.20. As an exhibition spectacle at the 2019 Super Bowl, Usain Bolt ran a 4.22 without even warming up. His time would have been a combine record. It's easy to understand why teams wanted to draft me. A championship-calibre 100-metre competitor could be murder on opposing defensive backs.

The interest was flattering, but I did not want to play football. If I became the number-one sprinter on the planet, the money would be just as good. Plus, football is played only in Canada and the United States, whereas sprinters travel the world and compete in front of sold-out 100,000-seat stadiums. Besides, I'd written off the idea of football back in high school. Did I want to spend my Monday nights worried a 250-pound linebacker was about to take my head off, sometimes in snow and freezing weather? I'd rather travel the globe and dine in Michelin-starred restaurants in Brazil, Australia, Japan, England, Czechia, Russia, Monaco, France, Italy and Switzerland. The choice to remain in track was a no-brainer.

And I would do it for Canada.

I had promised myself I'd enter the 1995 season with such dominance, I couldn't be refused by Athletics Canada again. I was good to my word.

My season began with a small meet. The LSU Invitational took place in April on very familiar turf: Baton Rouge, Louisiana. In the same city where I'd revamped myself, I set the Canadian record for the 100-metre dash. Bruny had previously owned the record with his 10.02 seconds, and in this event I posted 9.99. It was probably the easiest competition I ever ran. That's how in sync my body was at that moment.

There was not a lot of fanfare surrounding that meet. Certainly it wasn't on the average Canadian sports fan's radar. It was always like pulling teeth to get Athletics Canada to alert the Canadian media about significant results in track and field. But on this day, I wasn't letting it get to me. I knew there were bigger things in store. And the media found their own way to me. The CBC began to cover me prevalently, and the BBC was around, too. During one visit to Europe, I met a bunch of reporters who hailed from different countries around the world. Many of them expressed to me how much they enjoyed covering my events. They said they enjoyed conversing with me and appreciated my attitude and charisma.

I became even harder to ignore in July at the Canadian Track and Field Championships in Montreal. I owned the Canadian record, but now I wanted to set a new one on Canadian soil. I ran 9.91 seconds to beat my own record. Now I was not only the number-one sprinter in Canada, I was the number-one-ranked sprinter in the world, and I'd established that fact in front of Canadian fans.

The Canadian championships serve a double purpose. They serve as qualifiers for the national team that will represent Canada in the major international competitions, and the world championships were coming up in Gothenburg, Sweden. By the time my team and I landed there in early August, I'd lost only three competitions all season, and even those were podium finishes.

The top of the international field was on the track for the final: Frankie Fredericks, Linford Christie, Ato Boldon, Michael Marsh, among others. Bruny had won his semi-final and joined us for the deciding sprint. To his credit, he got as close to me as anyone that day, finishing second. It wasn't close enough. 9.97 seconds after the gun went off, I became world champion, which among other things earned me a custom Mercedes, shipped to Canada. I was the first Canadian to hold the title (and not lose it to disqualification). And before the games were done, I'd be relay champion, too.

I hadn't forgotten Stuttgart—watching the Team Canada coach beg athletes to run the relay for Canada while I was on the sidelines, badly wanting to be in that race. For me, the sport has always been about pursuing individual goals, and then putting the best team on the track to win medals. You lead by example by winning, then you make the decisions as leader. Not the other way around. My goal was now achieved, and my forewarning was now a reality: I was the number-one guy. Team captain. The athlete fans were coming to see and media were clamouring to speak with.

I have a friend who was playing at the time in the NBA. He had a championship ring. It was lavish, to say the least. When we received our rings for the relay championship, they were okay, a bit small. Jostens was one of my sponsors, and I went to them with an idea: big custom rings that we could show proudly in any company, the equal of any athlete's accomplishment. And that's what they made. I paid for these ones, though, all four.

I was the "king" now. Just like I said I was going to be. And my ultimate coronation was just around the corner.

CHAPTER 5

OLYMPIC HEAD GAMES

1996 WAS GOING TO be a whirlwind.

It was early in an Olympic year. Dan had been lured out of Louisiana by the University of Texas at Austin, and he made it a condition of accepting their offer that he could bring his chosen athletes west to train with him. They agreed, and it was off to Texas for me, Glenroy and a few other core athletes. That change alone shouldn't have thrown me off for long, and my coach could tell there was more than that small adjustment weighing on me. The Olympics would be taking place in the

United States that coming summer, so the spring was an important time for me to prepare.

I had competed indoors again that winter, always looking to make a statement to Athletics Canada. The results had spoken to my ascendance in the global sprinting hierarchy, exactly as I'd intended. In addition to being 100-metre world champion and the favourite looking ahead to the Atlanta games, I set the world indoor record in the men's fifty-metre with 5.56 seconds at the Reno Air Games in Nevada. That record stands to this day.

You might think that Athletics Canada and the COC would be warming to me by then. But I still felt like I was running into a headwind. I needed to rely on my own agents to report my competition results to the press by fax. I could get meetings with the IAAF or IOC, but Athletics Canada remained distant. I could thrive feeling like an outsider with them, though. I didn't really want to fit in, ever mindful that some of these people were the same officials who'd surrounded Ben Johnson when he'd been using steroids and then disowned him and any role they'd had in his career when his drug use was discovered.

Where I wasn't happy not fitting in was my own family. I wasn't seeing enough or hearing enough from my daughter, who was now one year old. I had signed a deal earlier with Bell Mobility, and the deal had included a cell phone with an Oakville local number so we could speak regularly. But nobody was answering when I called.

The Bell Mobility sponsorship was one of the more exciting I signed at the time. When the company went public on NASDAQ, I flew to New York to ring the bell at the opening of the trading day. While there, I did media, including morning television with

Regis Philbin and comedian Joan Rivers (Kathie Lee Gifford, Regis's long-time co-host, was off that day). I "raced" Regis on the street outside for a segment. He won, which tells you all you need to know about the segment. But all the fun the Big Apple could offer wasn't enough to distract me from the disconnect I was feeling with home.

Dan noticed I wasn't sleeping well. I finally told him what was bothering me, and he said I needed to "clean out my closet." He knew as a young father I'd made a big sacrifice to see my goals come to fruition. The upcoming months were critical to my life and career, and I couldn't afford to be operating with a cluttered abode, he explained. That was an eye-opening conversation for me. He was using a metaphor, obviously, but when I got home that night, I realized that taking him literally might help me sort things out figuratively.

I like everything in my home to have its place, and yet nothing seemed in order, which was not in my character at all. There were clothes and other things out of place. So, I went to work, systematically organizing the entire house.

As I cleaned up, I began to ruminate on my relationship problems and identify possible solutions. It was like I entered a trance. I moved on to the clothes that needed to go to the dry cleaner, putting them in a pile, and as I did that, my mind continued to sort out the problems I was having with the mother of my daughter. When I'd finished hanging up the clean clothes in the closet, I awoke from my meditative state. Thirty minutes had passed, and I now had a clean room and a clean mind.

I arrived the next day for practice in a refreshed state. I was out on the track, putting in work by myself, when I noticed something strange. I'd had my head down for a few minutes, and when I looked up, all of my fellow athletes had left the field. I figured it must be lunchtime or something and carried on with my business. When I looked up again, I spotted armed security guards nearby. A slender, middle-aged man began to move toward me. He was dressed in joggers, and he looked like he was here to work out, too.

As he got closer, he smiled and asked me who I was. "My name is Donovan Bailey," I responded. He genuinely had no idea who I was. Being Canadian and quite new to Texas, I didn't recognize him, either. Then he told me his name was George W. Bush and that he usually worked out here on Wednesdays. Given his tone, I interpreted his words to mean, *What are you doing here?* I was wondering the same about him.

"Perfect," I responded. "I work out on Wednesdays here, too."

Of course, I quickly realized that this was George W. Bush, the governor of Texas and son of former U.S. President George H. W. Bush. It turned out that he jogged about eighteen kilometres every Wednesday on campus, and people around there knew that late morning was *his* time. Dan hadn't mentioned it to me—maybe he wanted a good laugh. I didn't think any more of it, though, even if there were security staff visible on the surrounding buildings.

We became friendly over the course of his Wednesday visits and got to know each other quite well. We didn't go out for beers or anything so casual, but I did introduce him to the member of my team who handled my physical therapy and maintenance, chiropractor Dr. Mark Lindsay. I soon became "Fast Guy" and Mark was "Back-rub Guy." In later years, Mark took care of Bush during his presidential campaign. He always had a jolly demeanour, and I viewed him as a guy's guy. He was very direct and matter-of-fact, but he also had a sense of humour. He also displayed a level of swagger that I could appreciate as a Jamaican man. When he later became the forty-third president of the United States, I could admire and respect the kind of guy the country had elected.

In a few more months, he'd be able to point to the TV screen and say he knew me, too.

*

As we prepared for the Olympics, which would take place in Atlanta starting July 19, training became very particular to fine-tune my strengths and minimize my weaknesses. All that mattered now was being optimized for a few short days on a sweltering track in Georgia. I was laser-focused and my nutrition was on point. I was without injury, too, and really maximizing my time with Dan.

I'd won the 100-metre at the Canadian Olympic trials in Montreal, with a time of 9.98 seconds, securing my third consecutive national championship. Then, just weeks before the Games, I ran against a very competitive 100-metre field at a competition in Lausanne, Switzerland, when the pre-Olympics head games became more important than the competition itself.

Dan was at the venue, and when I arrived in the morning, he asked me, "What do you think we should work on today?"

The sprinting season is built in layers, and in the competitions leading up to the Olympics, we would focus on specific elements of my game. You had a lot of opportunities to face the same opponents before the big dance, and Dan's thought was that you didn't want to show all your cards before you needed to. Every athlete studies their opponents, and my competition and their coaches knew that I wasn't perfect off the blocks. They would try to hammer me on the start. They also understood that I was special at the fifty- to seventy-metre mark and could do things there that most other humans could not, so aiming to beat me in that segment was simply not an option. Consequently, Dan and I used a risk-reward analysis in choosing what to display during those pre-Olympics competitions and what needed more work. *Should we push during the whole 100 metres? Should we push certain zones of the 100 metres, like the start?* Sometimes our approach was simply about keeping the machine in one piece and not getting hurt.

By the time we got to that day in Switzerland, I could only respond to Dan's question about what I wanted to work on with a shrug. I wasn't sure. It was a genuine response; I really didn't know what we had left to fine-tune. He felt I should aim to be perfect at coming off the starting blocks, work on my drive phase and acceleration into top speed. That was it. He didn't want me to necessarily win the competition or set any records, just pay special attention to those areas and I'd be fine. That was our agenda. Any competition short of Atlanta was just training.

Namibian sprinter Frankie Fredericks was my main competition that day, and I was fired up to face him. In truth, I had added one more item to my race agenda that day: I wanted to mess with him.

A few weeks prior, on June 25 in Helsinki, Finland, Frankie had tried to toy with me. Our agents had agreed that he was going to sprint the 200-metre and I was going to sprint the 100-metre. We were going to face each other in the upcoming Olympics, so there was no need for us to square off now. I knew I'd be flat so soon after Montreal, so it was very important to my team that we know who was in the 100-metre. With Frankie sticking to the 200-metre, I would be the headliner. But then I got into the Finnish capital late.

In an ongoing pattern of frustrating behaviour, my agent Kevin Albrecht had scheduled an Air Canada TV commercial shoot with me from midnight through 9:00 a.m. the day I was flying to Finland. I'd just won the Canadian championship on June 21. Normally, I'd get right on a plane so I would have time before the next competition to acclimate to the local conditions. Helsinki was much cooler and wetter than Montreal in late June, and it was downright cold compared to Texas, where I lived and trained. Now, thanks to the commercial shoot, I'd be getting into Helsinki only the day before the 100-metre event. That left me no chance to practice in the local conditions or sleep off any jet lag.

I was pissed off. Because worse than any of this was having to work overnight. For an elite athlete, routine is a major part of training and maintenance. That includes getting enough sleep at regular times to ensure complete rest and recovery. My summer season was already tightly scheduled with a lot of travel; I needed to exercise absolute control over every minute of my day to stay competitive.

My agent booked the commercial, I showed up and did it, but I was furious.

When I arrived in Helsinki, I learned that Frankie had changed his mind. He was now running the 100. He had been in Finland for a week or more, training in the wet and cold, and was essentially lying in wait. Knowing I would get in so soon before the 100-metre and fresh off Canadian trials, he seemed to see it as a chance to mess with me ahead of Atlanta. He ran 9.86 for the win that day.

"You can have this one," I said to him. It was bravado, but I made a mental note to punish him at first opportunity. I skipped the post-race press conference and walked back to my hotel, simmering.

Now, back to Lausanne, where I got my chance to send a message of my own.

Dan asked me, "Do you want to break the world record today? Or do you want to wait for Atlanta?"

I thought about it, but not for long.

When the gun went off, Frankie was ahead, as always. He'd got out of the blocks first and stayed ahead for the first seventy metres. I then accelerated perfectly and pulled up to his shoulder. I looked over at him, then began to decelerate. I made sure he saw me and then allowed him to win. Mission accomplished.

The order in which we crossed the finish line was irrelevant. I wanted him to understand that my top speed was *always* going to outdo his. With the main event in the Olympics just around the corner, Frankie would be forced to line up in Atlanta haunted by the memory of a hollow victory in Lausanne. It was pure gamesmanship.

As I left the track, I had a new message for Frankie.

"You're going to be my rabbit."

In other words, like a greyhound on the fake rabbit that leads racing dogs around the track, I'd run him down in Atlanta and tear him apart.

I walked over to Dan, and his face was expressionless. That was normal for my coach. His cheeks were full of chewing tobacco, and as he worked that huge wad around, he spit out the words, "You just broke the world record."

I had finished with a 9.93 time that day. The world record for the 100-metre was 9.85, set by Leroy Burrell two years ago. So, I clearly hadn't broken any records. Yet, I knew exactly what Dan meant.

Coach had seen my acceleration and my execution to the seventy-metre mark. He knew that I had shut it down over the final thirty.

I told him with a smile, "I know."

＊

The most famous of footprints in Canadian track and field were ones I was unceasingly vigilant never to walk in.

The long shadow of the Ben Johnson steroid scandal hung over me more than most Canadian athletes, though. Like me, Ben was a sprinter who was born and raised in Jamaica before immigrating to Canada as a teenager. He was athletically gifted and began to make serious noise with his 100-metre dominance in the early 1980s. He set a world record in that event in 1987 with a time of 9.83 seconds that landed him the unquestioned title of World's Fastest Man. Ben became a celebrity at home and was honoured with the Order of Canada that year.

At the 1988 Olympics in Seoul, he lowered his time to an astronomical 9.79 and captured the gold medal—and glory for our country. But the celebration didn't last long. Within hours, he tested positive for steroids and was immediately stripped of the medal and the Olympic record time. Ben was suspended for two years and eventually stripped of his 1987 world record, as well.

Basically, Ben Johnson broke the collective heart of Canadian sports fans. These are people who invested time in him and in our sport. They cheered for him and took immense pride in his accomplishments. And it was all for nothing. His work had been a lie—or at least an enormous exaggeration of what Canadians had allowed themselves to believe.

When all of this was going down in the late 1980s, I was a keen observer, just like everyone else. It's not a stretch to say it was one of the biggest stories in the sporting world at the time. I mean, the 100-metre dash is among the most popular events on the planet. It's not confined to regions. If you break the world record in that competition, people from New Jersey to Jakarta are going to hear about it, and if you do it at the Olympics, they're probably all watching when it happens.

The Dubin inquiry was the Canadian government's investigation into the use of banned drugs by athletes. It was held in 1989, and while I didn't yet have both feet in the track and field world, I remember following the headlines.

As my own involvement in the sport accelerated, I heard constant rumblings about Ben. While the memory of the 1988 Olympics and its positive test followed me like a shadow, I tried to mentally separate my ambitions and developing brand from his tainted legacy. I viewed him as another insider in the Canadian track and field world. Like Bruny and Glenroy, he had come up through that system, whereas I did not. My interactions with officials were coloured by the fact that I was an outsider who had followed my own path to dominance. That mentality freed me from some of the baggage that Ben had left behind. At some stage, the system had left Ben to make decisions that would erase his accomplishments from the record books and throw the country into shame (if someone in the system hadn't actually *led* him to that decision). I owed that same system nothing. I was clean, and I had myself to thank for staying that way.

That historic baggage was always in the foreground, though—the media made sure of it. I was frequently asked about Ben from my first season in 1991 right up to the Olympics in 1996. There were some scrums where I fielded more questions about him than I did about my own performances. I believe that's where some people got the idea that I disliked him, that I viewed myself as the anti–Ben Johnson and that there was a rivalry between us. Sure, that would make for a compelling narrative. Hell, you could sell a lot of newspapers and magazines with that tale. However, it wasn't the case. I don't know the man, nor have I ever had a proper conversation with him, so how could I hate him?

I was busy rewriting the record books, undoing some of the stain he'd left behind. I was cleaning up the mess and helping Canada reclaim its place in track and field. As well, I was proud of the fact that I was a Black man creating positive news.

Ben and I were from different places in Ontario, different socio-economic backgrounds, different familial backgrounds with different support systems. Yet, we were both sprinters who had come to Canada from Jamaica, so a handful of reporters would always compare us. In interviews with me, they would circle back to Ben, and I felt that worked to sully some of the great individual and team accomplishments that I was part of. It took away from some of our successes when our very straight-forward victories should have been celebrated, without caveat. There were some occasions when I would even fight back and vent to reporters, asking why they didn't focus more on the good things that we were doing with Team Canada. "Why don't you focus on the team that's here?" I can recall saying in 1996, just ahead of the Olympics, telling the journalist of my irritation with being compared to "the ghost."

I always framed it for them through a hockey lens, since that was the sport that Canadian media dwelled on. Imagine if a team like the Montreal Canadiens won a championship, but the media continued to harp on some misconduct that a player on the team was involved in a decade before. Imagine if that misconduct, whatever it was, became an overriding factor in almost every conversation for the present-day Habs. Doesn't make sense, right? It would never happen, and yet, that's what I faced every time I was in front of a microphone or reporter's notebook.

I don't want to overstate the pressure caused by the Ben Johnson scandal. While being compared to him was especially frustrating to me in the lead-up to the 1996 Olympics, and I was honestly feeling some pressure to reclaim pride for my country, it wasn't overwhelming. The largest weight on my shoulders came from the fact that I was representing my parents, George and Daisy. I felt that pressure every time I laced up my spikes before a race. It was etched into my being at twelve years old, on the day that I rested my head in my mother's arms while she shed tears on our way to the airport in Kingston. I knew from that day forward, as I left her behind for my new life in Canada, that I had to honour her sacrifices. When you're armed with that kind of motivation, other sources of pressure don't feel so daunting. They're just business.

While I had grown tired of hearing Ben Johnson's name, I did empathize with his situation. Coming from a Jamaican family, I understood the full gravity of his sin. He'd brought shame to his household and culture. Over the years, I've had many conversations with my father about Ben, and my father has shared some very interesting and wise observations. One of them pervades my mind to this day: he told me to pay attention to how the media referred to Ben.

During the time frame that Ben was ascending into superstardom, he was hailed as a great *Canadian* hero. However, when all the controversy came to light, that moniker was replaced in news articles and reports with *Jamaican-Canadian*. My father was a smart man and immediately picked up on that shift in the language. When Ben was making everyone proud, the media happily dubbed him *Canadian*. When crime was attached to his name, all of a sudden his Jamaican heritage was slyly pulled into the conversation, even though by 1988 he had lived in this country for over a decade. I took that as though people couldn't openly call him the N-word, so diminishing his place in the country with microaggressions was their next best option. It was hard not to feel the distinct racial undertones, if you were paying attention. Ben was a national hero in 1987, but then he was just a Black man who ran, a Jamaican taking advantage of Canadian resources.

I thought that John Candy, the late great Canadian actor, of all people, described Ben's situation perfectly. He once told *US Magazine*, "At first, he was closely related to Sir John A. Macdonald, the first prime minister of Canada. The moment he was disqualified, he came from Jamaica."

My father and I did discuss the possibility that Ben was a victim of pressures and expectations he couldn't handle. Obviously, he cheated by ingesting banned substances. That's on him; he is responsible for that. Yet, at the same time, there's the distinct possibility that he was being used. He was the guy on the track who didn't ask questions, happy to be out there while people behind the scenes were making a lot of money off him and his name.

During our conversations about racism, my father never once spoke about the overt racism he faced when he arrived in Canada. I believe that he didn't want to place that kind of negativity in my mind. I once read that Herb Carnegie—a great Canadian hockey player who was denied entry into the NHL because he was Black—never spoke to his children about the harsh racism he endured, because he wanted them to believe without any doubts that they could accomplish anything they wanted in life. My father subscribed to that line of thinking. He preached the importance of hard work and said, "If you work your ass off and want to buy that house over there, you will buy that house over there. If someone's trying to stop you, go around them, over them or go beside them. If they want to stand in your way, go through them."

While my father didn't open up about the racist acts he encountered, he did enlighten me to the fact that passive-aggressive racism was part of life in Canada. Of course, I came to understand that myself over time. In the States, racism is often much more in your face. People don't like you because of your skin colour and they'll tell you that, or even worse, physically act on it. In Canada, racism is much more discreet. It's hyphenated. It's institutional. If someone doesn't like you because of your skin colour, maybe they won't approve your mortgage or they won't hire you for a job or they'll direct coded language toward you. Like hyphenating one's identity, for example.

This exact topic landed me in an interesting position in the summer of 1996, just before my much-anticipated Olympic competitions. In fact, *interesting* is an understatement. Perhaps I should say that it put a target square on my back.

Sports Illustrated reporter Michael Farber interviewed me for a story in the prestigious magazine while I was training in Texas, and when Canada's brand of racism came up during our discussion, I didn't hold back. My frank and honest answers were not received well by people in my home country, and that created a media firestorm.

These were my words as they appeared in the *Sports Illustrated* article: "'Canada is as blatantly racist as the United States. We know it exists. People who don't appear to be Canadian'— people of color—'don't get the same treatment. They associate you with your parents' birthplace or your birthplace . . . Look at our [sprint] relay. It's an issue . . . Will Canadians love a black

115

athlete? I hope so. I'm not an idiot. I know that people back home didn't get excited right after [Gothenburg]. They held their breaths.'"

By Gothenburg, I was referring to my becoming 100-metre world champion and our 4x100 relay gold-medal win at the 1995 world championships in Gothenburg, Sweden. That relay win was Canada's first relay gold in the world championships. That quartet was comprised entirely of Black men born in the Caribbean—Robert Esmie and myself are from Jamaica, Bruny hails from Haiti, and Glenroy was born in Trinidad.

I wasn't trying to be an activist—that's just not me. I take activism very seriously and leave that to the people who are better suited for it. Like my father, for example. Given his work with the Canadian Caribbean Association, I would consider him an activist, and I have great respect for the benefits he brought to his community.

When Farber asked me about racism in Canada, my answer contained my sincere thoughts. He asked and I answered just as I would in any conversation. To be clear, though, I did say, "Canada is *not* as blatantly racist as the United States." That's not backpedalling. To say that Canada's racism is *subtle* does not diminish its impact. Regardless, mainstream media outlets in Canada were upset, to say the least, that I had the audacity to come out and say such a thing. I remember hearing remarks that I was crazy, there was no such thing as racism in Canada and that we were in much better shape socially than our neighbours down south.

A subsequent quote from Carol Anne Letheren, former CEO of the Canadian Olympic Association and a member of the

International Olympic Committee, struck me as particularly harsh, despite the apparent effort to smooth over the controversy: "I'm surprised by Donovan's statement . . . If there's a tolerant country anywhere, it's Canada, a melting pot of many nationalities. Sure, we had some difficulties since the big influx of immigrants to Canada during the past 40 years, but we've always been able to deal with it. We have certainly not discriminated against any of our athletes, no matter where they were born. In fact, we're all looking forward to the 100-metre sprint in which Donovan Bailey and Bruny Surin are our big medal hopes. There's a special excitement in our camp that Bailey and Surin will do the job and we'll redeem ourselves by proving that the Ben Johnson affair was just a fluke." I was the number-one sprinter in the world, but she was reducing me to just another Olympian—one who needed to shut up and run.

When I arrived for the Games in Atlanta, I wanted to have a meeting with Canadian Olympic executives about my comments. I wasn't trying to lead a protest. I just wanted to shine a light on the fact that everything isn't rosy in Canada from a race perspective, and if people in charge continue to act like it is, that could be dangerous. People of colour are, in fact, treated differently in Canada, and we can't be blind to that. I call it "racism with a smile." A person can get an opportunity in Canada, sure, but there's a glass ceiling determining just how far they can go. And I say all that with the caveat that my experiences growing up in Oakville were quite positive. But my situation was the happy outlier. Some of my Canadian teammates endured much worse racism than I ever did. As the highest-profile athlete in the country, I was fine with taking the hit for my teammates in that regard, so long as it got the people running the program to take notice.

Canadian officials never once approached me to talk about my stance. They saw that I was putting myself out there with an opinion, and they left me stranded. I received no support, no guidance for handling the media attention, not even curiosity about why a fellow Canadian felt that way. Nobody took the time to ask. Maybe they were upset that I was rocking the boat, or maybe they genuinely didn't know how to handle the controversy, or didn't even think I was talking about them. However, several officials were nonetheless taking the time to downplay my opinion to the press. That was flat-out offensive and crystallized for me that in the grand scheme of things, I was just a number to our Olympic execs. I wasn't treated as a person whose thoughts and opinions were valued. They didn't even acknowledge the issue to me.

I never backed down from my stance. It's something I'm proud of to this day. But, I'll admit, it was jarring to watch the word *Jamaican* become affixed to the word *Canadian* when journalists mentioned me in print stories and on broadcasts.

I was once *Great Canadian Hero* Donovan Bailey. Now, all of a sudden, I had become *Jamaican-Canadian* Donovan Bailey.

Don't get me wrong—I'm a proud Jamaican. It's the land of my birth, and I will always have an unquestionable connection to the island. Just as most Canadians refer to themselves at times by their heritage—*I'm Pakistani, I'm Jewish, I'm Chinese, et cetera, et cetera*—I'm not trading in one aspect of my identity for another when I refer to myself that way. I had never worn a Jamaican uniform in international competition. I had done so for Canada, which made the backlash for my comment unbelievable to me.

The media was suddenly treating me in the exact same way they had treated Ben. Honestly, I would have preferred if they'd just got it over with and called me the N-word.

I have no doubt in my mind that the way I carried myself influenced the Canadian media's perception and portrayal of me. It was not just that I had made that comment about racism to *Sports Illustrated*. No, it was much more than that.

When I first burst onto the scene, I was looked at as a breath of fresh air on the Canadian track scene. I spoke my truth, was my authentic self and didn't put on a fake face in front of the cameras. What you saw was definitely what you got, and at first, that made me something of a media darling.

But along the way, I was deemed too outspoken, and it rubbed some people the wrong way. I began to see the word *arrogant* used to describe me. And when we talk about coded language with racial undertones, that's another key word. *Arrogant* is a euphemism for the N-word. When a white athlete speaks his mind, some will say, "Oh, he's confident." But if a Black person speaks in a similar fashion, *arrogant* appears. There is a history of characterizing outspoken men like me who speak their truth as arrogant, intimidating and threatening. Somehow, I thought I'd transcended that.

I saved some of the articles from those days to keep as a reminder. Also, because they genuinely bothered me. There was positive coverage of me in Jamaica, Asia, Europe, the United States and the United Kingdom, yet in my own country, I was facing a backlash. It was like the Canadian media was devouring the very scene that gave it a reason to exist. Someone once wrote that I was "un-Canadian." Really? What does that even mean? Don't work hard? Don't expect great results? Don't have high expectations? Don't speak the truth? Don't win? Is that un-Canadian? I can't describe how much that hurt me.

More recently, Alphonso Davies, the Canadian star of Bayern Munich football club in Germany, was criticized for allowing his wealth to show while playing with the Canadian national team and not always making himself available for media at the 2022 World Cup. He's a celebrity and wears expensive clothes and jewellery. His agent accompanies him to media availability when other players' do theirs alone, and he doesn't stop for the press every time they demand it. Good! He's one of the best soccer players in the world. That's what happens when you're the best (or should happen): you get paid, and your support team doesn't leave you alone in high-pressure situations. But there was the media, asking in a headline, "Is Alphonso Davies' celebrity a potential problem for Canada's men's World Cup team?"

That's some of the wildest coded language I've ever read.

Canada has a long history of Black athletes being kept in their place by administrators and coaches who didn't want them to win. One of the oldest and worst cases is Ray Lewis, who grew up in Hamilton, Ontario. His high-school coach was so dead set against him attending a major track meet in Philadelphia that he kept the whole team home when it threatened to boycott the meet unless the team included Lewis. Lewis's troubles continued when he was left off the 1928 Olympic team, again despite posting better times in the trials than some team members. He won the 1929 Canadian nationals but couldn't find a job, while the white members of the team were all hired as policemen, firefighters and other good work. The same people who encouraged Lewis to train in athletics turned their backs on him when he needed a paycheque. Lewis did win a bronze medal in the 4x100 relay in the 1932 Olympics, but lived out his working years as a railway porter.

Phil Edwards was on that same relay team as Lewis in 1932. He also won bronze in the 1500-metre, but the *Hamilton Spectator* newspaper ran a photo of Edwards following behind the triumphant Italian runner at the finish line. The caption beneath referred to Edwards only as "a colored boy from Canada." The Canadian media has always been quick to broadcast the glory of a Black athlete winning, and even quicker to demean one who disappoints.

I'd be remiss if I didn't mention Harry Jerome, bronze medal winner in the 100-metre at the 1964 Olympics in Tokyo. Harry Jerome asked questions. He challenged his coaches and drew those familiar criticisms about being "difficult," except I'm sure they were voiced even louder in his day. After he died, an annual meet was established in his name (the Harry Jerome International Track Classic), as well as the Harry Jerome Awards, highlighting excellence in African-Canadian achievement, and a statue erected in Vancouver's Stanley Park.

The idea of the prototypical Canadian athlete being someone who is buttoned down and self-effacing comes from my country's history with hockey. The pre-eminent players in that sport have always given quotes that are team-focused and never veer even remotely close to a bold statement. It's been like that for generations, and the power brokers in sports media have tried to fit all Canadian athletes—from every race and background—into that mould. But that's like jamming a square peg into a round hole. Hockey has predominantly been a white man's sport, and positions in Canadian sports media have been occupied for decades by white men, while the history of hockey in Canada was whitewashed and excluded the contributions of the Black Hockey League in Nova Scotia. You don't need me to do the math there.

Roberto Alomar was a superstar second baseman for the Toronto Blue Jays when they won back-to-back World Series championships in the early 1990s. He was born and raised in Puerto Rico, and like many Latin American baseball players, Alomar was dripping with swagger on the field. He played the game with a distinct flair. He was smooth to the point that Toronto sportswriters would sometimes question his dedication to the team. They thought his breezy, nonchalant nature was somehow indicative of his disinterest in winning. That was just straight up wrong. Alomar was a product of his environment, and that was something that many of the white media members who were drumming up these false narratives clearly didn't understand.

I had the same attitude and I attribute much of it to where I come from. I believe that Jamaicans possess a unique sense of self-confidence, and when it comes to athletics, that bravado is on overdrive. It is an area where we can fully express ourselves. I was in Kingston a few years ago for the annual Champs Jamaican high-school track and field meet, and watching the youth compete confirmed that to me. There was a twelve-year-old boy who had just won the 100-metre and was riding high. Someone stuck a microphone and camera in front of his face, and he said, with little expression, "I'm going to beat Usain Bolt's record." Then he proceeded to guarantee a few more achievements. I couldn't stop smiling when I saw that. The kid reminded me of myself. "Oh, hell yes," I told him before giving him a high-five.

My mentality was always that if I worked my butt off and expected to win, then why not say it? If I became a star, why should I hide from it? When I was a young boy, my father offered me a mantra to carry throughout my life: "If you're training, if you're studying, if you're doing anything to prepare yourself, why not talk yourself into being the greatest you? When you study, expect to get an A, or expect to win. Nothing less."

I've heard self-help gurus and motivational speakers ranging from Tony Robbins to Eric Thomas advise people to do the same. Maybe they use different words, but the general ethos doesn't vary much. Positive self-talk can do wonders for you. Of course, you have to put in your 10,000 hours of work to master a skill. But along the way, believing in yourself to that degree will take you to another level in your life and career.

Hip-hop artist Lil Wayne had a great quote in an interview I once read. When he was coming up in the industry, he dubbed himself "The Best Rapper Alive." Everyone knew that simply wasn't true. Jay-Z was the undisputed king and had used that phrase before Wayne did. But it didn't matter to Wayne, and when people criticized his declaration, he had a beautiful response. He said something along the lines of, "If I don't wake up every morning and tell myself I'm the Best Rapper Alive, then what's the point of even getting out of bed and making music? If I don't believe I'm the best, then what's the point?" It's almost as if Wayne took the words right out of my mouth.

CHAPTER 6

THE GREATEST

IT HAD FINALLY HAPPENED.

I laugh when I think back to my father's relationship with my track and field career. As upset as he'd been when I first told him about my decision to pursue sprinting full-time, we had bridged that gap considerably by the time I arrived in Atlanta in July of 1996 for the Summer Olympics. He was planning to make the trip to watch me compete, and with that I allowed myself to believe, at long last, I had convinced my father that setting my other business aside for track was really about embarking on a new kind of business for me. You'd think that being a favourite heading into the Olympic Games would settle an issue like that. But, in true George Bailey fashion, my father had some surprises in store.

My daughter, Adrienna, was going to turn two years old that August, and she was going to make the trip to Atlanta with her mother. When my father, ever the doting grandpa, found out that his granddaughter would be at the Olympics, he immediately made plans to spend time with her. And those plans, of course, superseded watching his son take a stab at creating history.

The 100-metre event featured several rounds that led up to the final—you don't just show up and sprint for the Olympic gold medal. You have to win or at least place well in each round to advance. With that in mind, I called my dad the day before my first competition and told him that I'd be sprinting at 10:00 a.m.

"The final road to becoming an Olympic champion starts early tomorrow," I said.

"Well, I made plans," he answered.

That stopped me in my tracks. What in the world could he have made plans for on such an important day?

"I'm going to take my granddaughter out for breakfast, because I promised her," he said. "Oh, and by the way, I won't be able to see you in the afternoon. I'm going to take her out for ice cream later on."

I couldn't help but chuckle at how unimpressed my father was by the height I'd reached in my career or the gravity of the moment in which I found myself. I smiled, grateful that he was spending quality time with my daughter. I've said I felt less pressure than some of my competitors to win because I had my family so solidly behind me. Well, I couldn't have that benefit and yet complain because my dad was putting family first at a moment like this. Even when he wasn't trying, George Bailey was teaching me how to be a better man.

My mother didn't make it to Atlanta. She hated to travel and preferred to stay in Jamaica, where she could follow along with the competitions in her own space and comfort. She was shy and didn't desire to be part of the hoopla. Sometimes you will see athletes' mothers in the media spotlight during the Games. That didn't suit my mom. And in the end, it was for the best. Because there would soon come a moment when I would be glad that my mother hadn't come to Atlanta, and at the same time, terrified for the safety of my father, my baby and her mom.

✳

Before Atlanta suffered a disaster, my Olympic dream nearly suffered one of its own.

In addition to regularly treating my back for problems caused by my slightly crooked spine, Mark spent a lot of time managing hip dysplasia on my left side. It was chronic and wouldn't ever go away, and it caused a slight hitch in my stride, which was never symmetrical as a result. He was in a running battle to keep my sacroiliac joint balanced and avoid a torsion—or twisting—at high speed that could injure my leg. At competition in Nice, France, two weeks before the Olympics, I tore my rectus femoris. That's a part of the quad muscles right where they meet the pelvis. That injury is particularly bad for a sprinter, because when our feet touch the ground, the quad stretches. That stretch brings the leg back from a stride. You don't lift the leg forward; it springs back as a reflex. You push and it comes back automatically. And I tore mine at the worst time.

A professional season can include as many as thirty competitions, and I was planning to race right up until Atlanta. But on July 10 in Nice, Linford Christie got out on me at the start of our final. It was one thing to throw the victory in Lausanne for the sake of getting in Frankie's head. I had no such plans for Linford. I caught the British sprinter at 95 metres and beat him with a 10.17, but at a significant cost. I had over-strided to catch him, and now my hip and quads were in ruins.

The tear had everyone asking questions: Would I tear it worse if I ran in Atlanta? Could I run in Atlanta at all? And could I make the start of the Games? The last question was certainly no. And that wasn't without consequences.

I had been asked to carry the Canadian flag into the brand-new Centennial Olympic Stadium during the opening ceremonies (the stadium later became Turner Field, home of the Atlanta Braves, and is now a college football venue). It is a huge honour just to be asked, and it spoke to the prominence I had developed on the Canadian sports landscape. Athletes chosen to carry the flag were usually entering the Games with a strong chance of medalling or else a hell of a backstory. I like to think I offered on both counts. But now, with a tear in my quadriceps, there was no way I could do it. Not only did I need to undergo treatment right up until my qualifying heats, I couldn't stand around for hours on the field during the long ceremony. My legs would seize up and all hell would break loose in my hip. I hated to decline, but Mark, Dan and I saw no choice.

It's a quirk of the Olympics that team doctors are chosen especially for that event. I'm sure the selection is an honour for them, too, but it means they don't always know the athletes they're treating. Team doctors thought I was out of the Games, period. So Dan and Mark called on a famous German sports doctor named Hans-Wilhelm Müller-Wohlfahrt (long-time team doctor for the Bayern Munich football club, as well as the German national football team). The three of them put together a rehab program that had me healing and training at the same time, so I wouldn't lose ground on my preparations for the Olympics.

I was in the pool, running with my feet off the bottom until the tear began to heal. Mark was putting me through acupuncture, soft-tissue release therapy, manipulating joints to activate functional movements that simulated running, gradually making the manipulations faster and faster as the healing could handle them. That was Mark's way: don't let the injury heal passively, but get my hip and quadriceps moving as soon as safely possible, and increase the intensity of movement every day (a method he would refine while working on a much more grave injury I suffered a few years later). We kept the therapy up until the day before Friday's qualifying heats and quarterfinals, when we had to leave Texas for Atlanta.

Dan thought that missing the early days of the Olympics meant I could lay low and stay away from the noise engendered by my comments to *Sports Illustrated*. I wasn't so concerned about that, but if Dan thought it was for the best, the idea probably had merit.

Under the midday sun on Friday, I edged out Japanese sprinter— and another of Dan's pupils—Nobuharu Asahara to win my first heat by .04 of a second. The top three finishers advanced, so the close finish was irrelevant. I didn't need to break any records this early. Even with my leg so fresh from injury, I was too confident to worry about impressing anyone at this stage. I finished my quarterfinal that evening .02 seconds behind Linford Christie. Again, with the top four advancing, it was little more than practice—and reassurance that my quadriceps wasn't going to let go of my hip.

It would be nice to end the story of the day before my record-setting win on a high note. Nothing could ever be that simple. As I was trying to settle into a quiet evening at the residence where the relay team was staying, we had a knock at the door. The Canadian team had decided to administer last-minute un-scheduled drug tests for us. They just couldn't believe we were doing as well as we were. Bruny was also running in tomorrow's semi-final and had high hopes of joining me in the final.

I was deeply annoyed. This wasn't WADA (World Anti-Doping Agency), as you might expect. Even they wouldn't chase us down at our residence the evening before the biggest race of our lives to piss in a cup. No, it was the COC, our own team, so unwilling to believe that its athletes had come this far without cheating that it would send people to our doorstep unannounced at an hour when our mental focus should have been a team priority. This was inexcusable.

Disappointed but too focused on the next day to let it get the better of me, I went to bed. Just as well. Bigger forces would rattle us all in the morning.

———

Childhood in Jamaica was idyllic, and school always came first.

With my mother and older brother O'Neil.

Our house on Woburn Crescent.

Grade ten, after joining my father and O'Neil in Oakville.

Making friends as a camp counsellor, my first job.

Dressed for success on Bay Street, before I got serious about an athletic career.

At twenty-one, when I was getting back to the track but only part-time.

It looks painful because it was. Mark Lindsay kept my body in winning condition.

At the university track in Austin with my coach Dan Pfaff.

Dan analyzing every tiny motion for optimal performance.

Celebrating with Bruny Surin after finishing 1–2 at the Canadian nationals in 1995.

Crossing the finish line for gold at the 1995 World Championships.

The relay team with coach Mike Murray, celebrating our gold at the 1995 worlds.

Atlanta, 1996. 100-metre world champion, and now world-record holder and Olympic champion, too.

The Atlanta relay team at our residence in Buckhead. I'm on the left, beside Carlton Chambers, our host, Bruny and Glenroy Gilbert.

It's relay gold for Canada in Atlanta.

Bruny, Glenroy, me and Carlton, very happily awaiting our Olympic medals. Brothers for life.

Celebrating with a parade in my hometown of Oakville.

Oakville named a street and park for me. High honours.

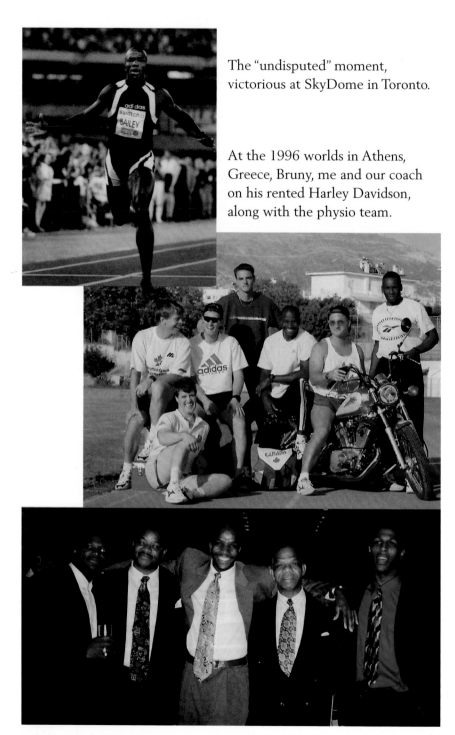

The "undisputed" moment, victorious at SkyDome in Toronto.

At the 1996 worlds in Athens, Greece, Bruny, me and our coach on his rented Harley Davidson, along with the physio team.

The Bailey boys. My cousin Andrew, Uncle Lester, me, Dad, and my brother O'Neil.

Horsing around at the track with Glenroy, my greatest relay teammate.

Waving to the crowd at my final Harry Jerome Classic in Vancouver.

Music is my happy place and was always part of my training regimen.

My father prioritized family. Here with my daughter, Adrienna.

My first official visit to Canadian Olympic Committee headquarters in nearly two decades, with good friend Sunir Chandaria and committee CEO David Shoemaker.

A blessed son. With my beloved parents, George Bailey and Daisy Lewis.

Saturday morning was surreal. I don't think I could describe it any other way.

The team wasn't staying in the Olympic Village—that would have been too distracting. Instead, we were situated in an upscale northern district of Atlanta called Buckhead. The Royal Canadian Mounted Police (RCMP) were on guard around the houses. The location isolated me from the city and the Games whenever I wasn't actively participating. I woke up the morning of the semi-finals and final at around eight. The competitions were taking place in the evening. I headed downstairs to get a bagel and an omelette for breakfast.

Dan, my coach, walked in as I was chowing down on my eggs. He had a stern look on his face. Remember, this is a man who was expressionless 99 percent of the time, so the tiny hint of emotion etched around his eyes alerted me that something was wrong.

"There was a bombing," he said, taking a seat across from me. "We don't know if the Games are going to continue."

"You cannot fuck with me today," I responded.

I was laser-focused and figured he was trying to test me. Perhaps he wanted to see if I was firmly enough in my zone? My curt remark was both a declaration of my resolve and a demand that he stop trying to shake it.

I looked him straight in the eyes. Dan was always better at saying things without saying them. He broke his gaze, got up from his chair and walked to the television. He turned it on, then walked out of the room.

I turned to the news. *Oh my God.*

A pipe bomb concealed in a knapsack had exploded amidst a crowd in Centennial Olympic Park, killing one person and injuring 112 others. A photojournalist then died of a heart attack while rushing to cover the tragedy. Years later, it came to light that a man named Eric Rudolph was responsible. He also set off bombs at abortion clinics in Birmingham, Alabama, and Atlanta, as well as a gay nightclub in Atlanta.

Dan walked back in, and it's a good thing he did. It was the only time in my entire existence when I completely panicked. My stomach was churning—*112 people injured, plus two dead*. Just thinking of the people suffering as they lay wounded on the street and sidewalks even as we sat in that comfortable, protected house shook me. I peppered him with questions about the tragedy, but he didn't have all the answers. As my mind began to process what had happened, I began to worry about my competitions. It might sound trite in the context of all that suffering, but you don't train your mind and body for years toward a day like July 27, 1996, and lose your focus for long.

"What's going to happen?" I asked him. "Are we even going to continue?"

"Well, we've done all the work," he responded. "We're here and we're prepared. None of this is in our hands right now, so we will have to wait and see what the governing bodies have to say."

His words really served to calm me and slow my racing heart. It was out of our hands. Yet again, Dan had proven our complete synergy. He always knew what to say to me and how to say it. It was like he was living in my head. I went back to my bedroom to try to sleep off the lingering pangs of anxiety, and when I woke up, Mark gave me a massage and flushed the remaining nerves from my body.

A few hours later, we got word that the games would go on. The RCMP escorted us to the stadium, and there was an eerie feeling penetrating the air. Security was in front of my car and behind us. Everyone seemed to be in a fragile state. We were nervous that we could be heading into more attacks. I noticed how tense everyone was when I arrived at the venue.

Readying myself to race became a matter of compartmentalizing the horror. To sprint in the wake of a tragedy like that, I had to dig deep and focus on my job. By now I had some experience erasing outside factors from my sightlines during competition. All I could control was my preparations and what my legs did on the track for the duration of 100 metres. When you simplify a day's work in that manner, focus becomes much easier. Dan had always lauded my ability to "flip a switch." He used to joke that months before a competition, my mind might wander all over the place, but as we drew closer to the main event, I'd become like a heavyweight boxer. My sleep patterns, diet and attention to detail would naturally sharpen and enter a tunnel.

Dan, of course, deserves some credit for this focus, since he was the mechanic who could expertly tune my sprint engine. We had a conversation about executing in the semi-finals and, following that, the finals. Both sprints would be held that same day, a few hours apart.

He brought up my recent event in Lausanne—the one where he remarked to me that I had broken the world record based on my first seventy metres. He had actually asked me if I wanted to shock everyone in the Olympic semis or wait until the finals to enter the record books. He grinned as he asked, and I believe he already knew what my answer was going to be.

By Saturday evening's semis in Atlanta, the top competitors had distinguished themselves. I was on the track with Frankie Fredericks, the American Michael Marsh and Michael Green of Jamaica, among others. I had a false start. If I did it again, I'd be disqualified. That rule has since changed; sprinters these days don't get a second chance. Guys too often would use an intentional false start as a way to mess with their competition, staring them down as they walked back to the starting blocks. A mental and physical reset is needed after a false start, and the more mentally tough guys could really lean on the others in those moments (I'd once said to a competitor in a moment like that, "Don't worry, it'll be over soon"). Others could be totally thrown off their game by too many false starts.

Fortunately, I got away clean on the second try, accelerated well and shut it down once I knew I'd finish in the top two. I'd run a 10.00. Frankie ran a sub-ten to take the semi-final, but it was all according to plan. I didn't care what my time was.

Remember that race in Lausanne, and the message I'd sent there to Frankie? Well, in Atlanta, he and Ato Boldon of Trinidad and Tobago were the only sprinters to run sub-tens in qualifying. Top guys usually don't show their best stuff so early, for the sake of avoiding injury and not showing their hand. My two top opponents had just shown me they could compete, but if they were really ready to win they shouldn't have felt the need to show me anything.

My only real concern in the semi-final had been to secure a good middle lane for the final. Remember the energy vortex I mentioned? Well, I certainly got that when I was handed lane five—smack in the middle of the action. Perfect.

There were about ninety minutes between the end of the semis and the scheduled start of the gold-medal event. I headed to a back room, had a few acupuncture needles placed on my legs and nodded off for a twenty-minute power nap on the massage table. When I awoke, my resting heart rate was around thirty-eight beats per minute. I was very, very calm and confident. Dan had one final message for me, and his words acted almost like a muscle relaxant to my entire body: "Hey, man, you've done all the work. This is for you to lose. So go get it."

About forty-five minutes before my competition, I headed to the practice track and began to slowly warm up my body. Then, as we entered the stadium I gazed into the crowd and took deep breaths, savouring the moment. The here and now. The sea of people in the stands resembled an abstract painting with thousands of little white and brown dots. It was quite beautiful. Later, when I had time to reflect, I was struck by the contrast between 1991 and 1996, how I'd grown as a competitor. When I'd competed in Havana at the Pan American Games, the packed stadium had left me unhinged. Fast forward to Atlanta, and being in front of thousands of amped-up spectators didn't raise my heart rate by one single BPM.

I was in my zone. All the buzz and chatter from the crowd was muted to me, but if a pin were to drop somewhere on lane five, I would have heard it. I was unaware of my competitors, and when I peered out at my lane, it almost looked like there were walls on both sides, keeping me from noticing anybody else. I remember smiling to myself and thinking, *This is crazy.*

The actual competition was bizarre, with a whopping three false starts, two of them belonging to Linford Christie. He was disqualified and that was a complete shock, given that the British sprinter was the defending champion after winning 100-metre gold in 1992. Of course, he appealed for a review and that caused a long wait time for the rest of us. Dan had prepared me for this during our training in Austin. He predicted that there were going to be some false starts, and when it played out in reality, I remembered his advice. "Whatever happens, always reset," he warned me. Heeding his words, I went back to my starting block and did some jumping jacks. It was a way, according to Dan, to reload my spring, so I could explode when the dash finally began. I didn't pay much attention to Linford, who was understandably making a fuss on the track. His appeal didn't prove successful, and he was ultimately ruled out.

Finally, we got our fourth try. This time it was real, and boy, was it bad for me. I had a horrific start off the blocks. Absolutely horrific. Because I didn't want to false start myself, I sat back in the blocks for a millisecond too long. The gun went off and I thought, *Oh shit*. In one of the false starts, I'd actually got away so cleanly, Dan told me later he thought I could have run a 9.6. In my final days of practice, he'd actually expected me to run a 9.6 in Atlanta. Now I was behind pretty much everybody. But I had done my homework. I knew that my responsibility in that moment was to stay relaxed. If I did, everything would take care of itself.

Dan had actually gone over the possibility of a false start like this during our training. We practised what I would do if I was the last out of the blocks. I would need to regroup and basically use one-thousandth of a second to correct my mistake and continue on my trajectory. I had given up roughly 1.5 metres to the rest of the guys, and my task was to regain that, plus more. I thought to myself, *Just relax. Just relax. Just relax.* Meanwhile, my body took over in a purely reactive state.

The first thirty metres were objectively horrible, but my middle forty were probably the best I've ever sprinted. I gained extensive ground and accelerated to a pace of 12.1 metres per second at the sixty-metre mark. I knew I had won the competition by the time I reached seventy metres. I saw the finish line coming up and tried my best to relax. I tightened up a little bit by the ninety-five-metre mark, but by then, it was over.

I finished first with a time of 9.84 seconds.

A new world record.

The title of World's Fastest Man.

The greatest sprinter in the history of the world.

My very first Olympic gold medal.

A new, clean narrative for my country.

People ask me all the time what popped into my mind as I crossed the finish line. It's funny. There were bonuses in my sponsorship contracts tied to winning, as well as breaking the world record and the Canadian record, which I had previously set at 9.91. I was so mindful of my athletic career being a business that once I realized I had broken the record, dollar signs flashed across my mind. *Cha-ching!* I had more than a few sponsors at the time, and winning gold meant a lot of money was coming my way. In the middle of all the hoopla, I was thinking about contracts and bonuses.

The next thing on my mind was beating everyone else and becoming the champ. Frankie Fredericks finished second (9.89

seconds) and Ato Boldon of Trinidad and Tobago secured the bronze (9.9).

Setting the world record was a distant third to come to mind. That may seem odd, but hear me out: When you're an Olympic champion, nobody can ever take that away from you. If you win Olympic gold, it is accepted that you were the best on the planet during the time you competed. Nobody could touch you. World records, on the other hand, are transient. As time passes and the science behind training and nutrition advances, new world records are inevitably set. Someone is eventually going to better your time.

If you go back and look at the video of me immediately after the race, you will see a man beaming with pride. I grabbed a Canadian flag, wrapped it around my shoulders and strolled proudly along on a victory lap. It was a very sweet moment. I've always had the ability to be in the moment and soak up the sights, sounds and feelings in the immediate wake of competitions. The stadium was roaring, in part because there were so many Canadians there. Atlanta was a short flight away for many of my compatriots. It felt like a home crowd, and seeing those red-and-white flags, I knew I was representing a nation. The gravity of what I'd just done for my country wasn't lost on me. I was also aware that, even though I wasn't wearing the Jamaican colours, many people from my birth island, along with Yardies across the world, were rooting for me. I was representing a vast number, and it meant a lot.

Over the years, I have met people who have graciously shared stories about where they were during the race. People told me that their wedding and graduation ceremonies were paused so people could watch. Some have told me that they named their sons "Donovan" or their daughters "Bailey."

Wow.

I've heard stories of women naming their pets after me and men doing the same with their boats. One person even dubbed their ride *The 9.84*. And these were people of all colours. I've noticed as the years have passed that there was no racial divide among my fan base. I didn't notice it in my younger days, but I now realize that my work meant different things to different people. Each fan absorbed my story and made it their own. Just thinking about that makes my heart want to burst with gratitude.

People have remarked to me that it's possible my accomplishments helped many Canadians understand what this occasion could mean to their country. My parents raised me in a way that enabled me to see the importance of having a microphone placed in front of me. You never knew who was watching and inferring certain ideas based on what they saw. So, I wanted the audience to view a man who was eloquent, confident and worthy to be an ambassador of his sport and our country.

As I walked around the track in Atlanta, draped in the Canadian flag, I was also representing my family. My gold medal was partly a by-product of their work—the choices and sacrifices of my mother and father, along with the time that my extended family and friends back in Canada and Jamaica put into me from my youth to the present. There is footage from that victory walk of me shouting out "Uncle Keith"—an homage to one of the most beloved members of my family.

Minutes later, though, my immense joy turned into engulfing sadness. The day that I won the gold medal was about to turn into one of the saddest days of my life.

Once I left the track, I felt the need to call Uncle Keith and share my joy with him. I managed to squeeze in a moment just before my media availability and dialed his home number in Markham, Ontario, where he'd moved to from Florida. He'd been one of my very favourite people and co-author of some of the most enjoyable memories from my time as a youth in Jamaica. Our relationship embodied total freedom, and it had stayed that way into my adulthood. That's why I was so distraught by what happened next.

When I called Uncle Keith's home following my gold medal win, a family member answered. I asked to speak with Uncle Keith, and she told me that he had passed away. Keith's wife, Aunt Yvonne, was in the background and became livid that I had found out. She didn't want me burdened by the tragic news on the biggest day of my life. I had known Uncle Keith was suffering from pancreatic cancer but did not know the status of his condition. I thought he had much more time.

I learned that he had watched all of my Olympic races up until the previous night but did not make it into the morning. He missed my gold medal victory, which hurt me in a way that is hard to describe. My father had been at the event, as were many of my close friends who had made the trip from Oakville. My Uncle Keith, though, never lived to see that moment.

I've gone back and looked at the video of me shouting out his name. And it still pains me to know that I did so thinking that he was watching me on TV. Instead, he had already left this world, but I know now that as one of my guardian angels he had been cheering me on.

A bomb at the Games, a major injury barely recovered from, a death in the family—my time in Atlanta wasn't peaceful, and it was further complicated by issues behind the scenes.

I had two sets of agents: Kevin Albrecht handled areas like sponsorship, while Mark Block and Ray Flynn took care of dealings specific to track and field. Kevin worked for International Management Group (IMG), and we hadn't been seeing eye to eye for a while. I was a creature of habit and structure, and had crafted a daily routine with Dan that ensured my optimal performance in competition. In order for my body to work as I expected, I had to treat it as it expected. The closer I got to a competition, the more important my schedule became. Kevin didn't seem to understand that or care, and wasn't taking my schedule into account when arranging business commitments for me, such as advertising shoots. A few times in 1996, he had booked me to film a commercial through the night, from 12:00 to 9:00 a.m. At that point, I was deep into my training and, of course, didn't want to deviate.

I was building a strong brand and viewed myself as Bailey Inc. My employees worked for me, and I was the one who gave instructions. It wasn't the other way around. My agents had a responsibility to recognize my training and competition schedule and to slot my commitments around that. I was the talent, and I needed to do what I needed to do to remain the talent.

As the 1996 Olympics were approaching, my contract with IMG was coming up for renewal after the Olympics. I hadn't given any indication that I was interested in re-signing with the agency, since I wasn't happy with what Kevin was doing. Apparently, around this time, my other agents, Mark and Ray, heard from Kevin that he had research that concluded I wasn't going to win the 100-metre, so he wasn't going to represent me any longer.

Mark and Ray debated telling me about that slight and waited until after I'd won the 100-metre gold to do so. Kevin called me, gold undisputedly hanging from my neck, to tell me he had secured $50 million in contracts for me. I was so livid that he would have the balls to reach out to me after saying he didn't think I'd win.

"No!" I shouted. "You're fired. You no longer represent me."

This wasn't going to be good for my soon-to-be-former agent. If his bosses saw my success in Atlanta and asked him, "Hey, Donovan Bailey is the biggest track star in the world right now—why is his contract extension not in place?" Kevin would have some explaining to do.

For years after Atlanta, I faced a constant battle with the perception that I was difficult to deal with. This reputation made it easy to just say no to me, a convenient excuse to leave me out. More headwinds coming my way, headwinds I was feeling but nobody else was seeing or not seeing by design. Maybe it was a way for IMG to avoid blaming its own people for my departure. But the exclusion of Donovan Bailey had begun, and I wasn't even done competing yet in Atlanta.

*

I won gold on Saturday night, and by Tuesday I was right back to work with Team Canada. As much as I was grieving and muddling my way through an intense mix of emotions, I was the leader of the men's 4x100-metre squad, and we had a job to do.

We would run the relay in the same order that had won us the world championship. That order went as follows: Carlton Chambers was the leadoff man, followed by Glenroy, Bruny on the third leg and myself as the anchor. (Carlton competed in the early rounds but sustained a groin injury that prevented him from running in the final race. He would be replaced by Robert Esmie.) After our relay training camp earlier in 1996, we were all extremely familiar with our individual roles.

The air around our relay squad was thick with competitive angst. Throughout camp and now the final preparations, we could be friendly with each other but, at the same time, fierce killers when it came to individual success. The dynamic on the relay team is a lot like I imagine it is in golf's Ryder Cup, an event where highly competitive individuals must play as teams, under their captains' guidance, for a single victory. The biggest egos have to be put in check without being snuffed out.

Fresh off breaking the world record, I was wired to perfection, from an athletic perspective. My cadence, rhythm and bounce were at their peak. My technical mechanics were efficient and utterly flawless. I'd proven myself top dog after my historic victory. Whatever they felt about that would have to be placed on the back burner so that we could bring another gold medal home to Canada—or four, to be precise.

During our practices, Bruny was having some difficulty handing the baton to me in our prescribed receiving zone. That is the most crucial element in a relay competition. It doesn't matter if each athlete sprints the leg of their life, if they fumble the hand-off, then the whole team's race is over. Both men are in flight when the transfer occurs, too, and it has to happen in the zone or disqualification is immediate. There is the smallest space for error. And in one heat, we used all of it.

The Americans were taking the qualifying races by at least half a second over everyone else. They were looking like the team everyone thought they were. Smooth, fast and dominant. I didn't care. The rest of our team thought we could be competitive with them, but their view fell short of my own. I wasn't interested in the winning history of the American relay team. We were going to beat them. Period. The only thing standing in our way was the weak hand-offs that had been plaguing our practice runs.

The speed of the incoming runner has to connect momentarily with the speed of the runner ending his 100 metres for a smooth transition. But as the number-three runner, Bruny wasn't catching me as I took off to meet his speed, take the baton and then accelerate into my own run. I'd had to slow down in order for him to get the baton in my hand before my back foot left the receiving zone. In practice, I said I'd shorten the receiving zone so he would have a chance to hand off the baton before I hit top speed. Maybe it was an ego thing, but he said no. He'd get it to me. And then in a qualifying heat, he almost didn't.

As Bruny approached at top speed, I took off from the tape on the track where I started my leg. As I accelerated, I could see the line at the end of the receiving zone approaching. Quickly. Time slows in those moments and thoughts quicken. I pictured the line in long jump, or the free-throw line as I ran down a basketball court on my way to a flying dunk. If I hit that rapidly approaching line without the baton in my hand, our time in Atlanta was over. That is not what a sprinter is supposed to be thinking about in a relay. You're accelerating and waiting for the command—"Stick!"—prompting you to reach back and take the baton. It should just be there. That's why we practised.

Most of me was out of the zone. The smallest fraction of my back foot was still in the box when I finally got the baton: officials had to review the tape.

The hand-off was judged to be legal. Barely. We were not disqualified.

This could not continue.

I pulled Bruny aside. "Dude, I'm on next level," I said to him. "Can you turn this up? Can you bring it?"

To his credit, Bruny took ownership. "No, don't worry," he responded. "I got it. I'm gonna bring it."

I believe it's important to clear the air about my teammates. I never considered any of them rivals, despite what the media may have reported. Bruny was from Quebec, and I know there were some people in the French-speaking media who considered him *their* guy. They backed him in their articles and opinion pieces, taking digs at me along the way. I shut it all out and never worried about what was happening in the careers of other sprinters—and that included international competitors like Frankie Fredericks, Linford Christie and Ato Boldon. I had a very healthy respect for anyone who brought it on the track; I didn't need the emotion of considering them *rivals* in order to bring my best against them.

As for my team, we were there to do a job together. I would make sure that I executed my role. And I knew that if I did that, my teammates would, in turn, feel more confident in their own roles. Having the world champion, world-record holder and freshly crowned Olympic champion on their side allowed my team an elevated sense of bravado and the space to focus on their individual tasks. No one needed to overextend himself and try to play the hero. That was my job.

The inspiration wasn't all going one way. Watching Glenroy, my friend and training partner, go about his business in practice gave me comfort in our chances. His role as the second leg in the relay was crucial, and I genuinely feel he was and remains the most underrated sprinter in Canadian history. He possesses an incredible work ethic and was gifted with immense talent. Unfortunately, he could never quite put it together in individual competition. You put a baton in his hand, though, and Glenroy produced magic. He was driven by a heavy sense of responsibility towards his teammates, which he didn't put on himself the same way in solo sprints. In a relay, I would match him up against any single person in the world, past or present.

On the day of the final, we were hearing a lot of smack talk from the Americans. In a closed corridor with the other athletes during the warm-up session, Americans Jon Drummond and Dennis Mitchell were running their mouths. Based on their individual 100-metre times, the U.S. relay team was the fastest in the world. The media had built them up to be untouchable, and their four sprinters bought into that narrative. They were debating who was going to win the silver medal—as if their gold was already in the bag. I understood what they were doing, though. No harm, no foul. Back then, we weren't friends with competitors in the same way you see in today's track and field world. No, we competed like boxers, and there was mental manipulation attached to it. American coach Charles Greene famously claimed, "You can take it to the bank" that his team was going to win.

I don't know how the other teams in there—the Brazilians or Ukrainians or any of the other relay teams—took the American head games, since we were the only other English-speaking nation in the final. But even assuming that the Americans were directing their intimidation tactics at us, my teammates and I weren't fazed. I admired Carl Lewis, but when I heard he was lobbying to compete in the relay, I said in a press conference of my own, "Carl is way smarter than that to step on that track. He knows what's up."

Each of us was true to form that day in Atlanta. We were given lane six, while the U.S. sprinters occupied lane four. Robert—who went by the nickname "Blast Off" and even had those words shaved into his head—led off against Jon Drummond and then handed off to Glenroy, down by a tenth of a second. Glenroy produced a second leg that was flawless, everything I knew we could expect from him, and overtook Tim Harden to give us a slight lead. Bruny maintained the lead against Michael Marsh, the 1992 200-metre Olympic champion, before handing the baton off to me—perfectly. He knew the race was over as soon as the baton was in my grasp and put his hands up in the air to celebrate. As I added to our lead over the rest of the field, including American anchor Dennis Mitchell, who had watched me win gold a week earlier from fourth place in the 100-metre final, Bruny began to pump his right fist. It was all a little premature, but I heard him say later that he was so excited that he wanted to run to the finish line, too. I knew it was over, and before I even crossed the finish line, I put my right hand in the air, closed my fist and pointed to the sky with my index finger to emphasize that we were number one.

Our time of 37.69 set a Canadian record, and the fact that it came against the Americans, who had won fourteen of the eighteen prior Olympic gold medals in the event, in their own house, made it even sweeter. It was the second time in seven days that I had crossed the finish line to secure a gold medal. Days later, I watched a replay of the broadcast and heard the announcer, Don Wittman, shout, "If you're a Canadian, you have to love Saturday nights in Georgia." I thought that was brilliant.

With the heightened sense of calculation that I possessed during those days of peak competition, the win was just another day at the office. However, part of me was overjoyed to help my teammates Robert, Glenroy, Bruny and Carlton—who also received a gold medal for his participation in the earlier rounds—achieve something that would be attached to their names for the rest of their lives. It would be the only Olympic gold that any of them would win. It had been a lifelong ambition for them, and as the king, I had made it possible. Every athlete had had his own unique route to get to where they were, but now the hope was that they could all profit in some way from this and use it to help them grow their careers. I did feel the responsibility to be a leader and a team player, in that sense. I trusted those men—I knew they were good people and that they were clean, with no history of PED use. Because of that, we could collectively sell our sport in Canada and across the world as role models.

For me, personally, this win also added a neat bookend to my issues with all the Canadian officials who had left me off relay teams. Remember when I told Glenroy, "When I'm the king here and I run shit, this will never happen"? Well, you can imagine the vindication I felt when we threw our arms around each other on the track in the heart of Georgia.

I found it incredibly satisfying that Molly, who had been my sounding board during those earlier days and had given me such good advice, was one of our coaches. After all she'd done for me, I was glad that she had a front-row seat to our victory.

She and I had a conversation in Atlanta that reflected on our past chats. We also casted forward, thinking about where my career would take me next. The work wasn't done, Molly said. She wisely cautioned me to be careful what I wished for, because when I got it, I'd be exposed. She said I was more vulnerable at this point than ever, because the spotlight was fixed on me. To hammer her point home, Molly brought up the popular North American tradition of Groundhog Day. Just like that famous groundhog in Punxsutawney, Pennsylvania, I had emerged from the shadows to make my declaration, drawing a world of attention and hope to myself in the process. Now, spring had sprung, and the new season had arrived in my career. The question was: How was I going to deal with it?

———

For all the glory and sadness I'd experienced in Atlanta, my time at the Olympic Games ended on a high note—the highest, in fact. A dream came true. For my first and only time, I met Muhammad Ali.

What can I say about the man? I looked up to my father, and my father looked up to Ali. As a boy in Jamaica, I had hung off every word of his matches on the radio, and I'd sat with my father glued to the TV in Oakville, watching Ali fight and talk like nobody ever had. He shaped my entire attitude to my sporting life, and he had just lit the Olympic cauldron at the opening ceremony in Atlanta. That deed alone was a standout moment of strength, as he had done it in front of the whole world despite his hands shaking from the debilitating effects of Parkinson's disease. I hadn't seen him do that in person, even though I'd been asked to carry the Canadian flag into the stadium. I'd been stuck in Texas—battling with that adductor injury that two weeks before the Games was preventing me from even walking—and watching the opening ceremonies from home.

I didn't think I would ever get the chance to meet *The Greatest* (the title of his autobiography). I was a Canadian sprinter, while he was a living legend. But fate intervened. One day in Atlanta, I heard he was going to be at a hotel in the Olympic Village. I happened to be nearby for a meeting. No way was I letting even the slimmest of chances pass me by. I made the split-second decision to show up where he was scheduled to be. And there he was.

I was wearing my Team Canada track suit, and he was wearing an Atlanta Olympics T-shirt and white chinos. I was mesmerized as I walked up to him. I felt like a three-year-old.

He shook my hand and said, "Hello, champ." I couldn't believe it. Muhammad Ali not only knew who I was, but he was aware of my accomplishments at these Games. That was truly surreal.

I smiled and immediately responded, "No, *you're* the champ," which brought a hearty laugh from him. That was the extent of our exchange. It was short but . . . it was Muhammad Ali! I'll cherish that memory until the end of my life.

In later years, I was able to reflect on that meeting and the many ways in which the man and his story resonated with me. Ali had been hated by some people in the American public for his stance on race and against the war in Vietnam. Yet, in the end, he was beloved by those same people. My public and dis-puted stance on racism in Canada did not carry anything close to the heightened stakes that he dealt with in the 1960s and '70s. All I did was point out that racism existed, while Ali, on the other hand, was among the highest-profile African-Americans in the civil rights movement and had been willing to go to prison as a conscientious objector to the war. Nonetheless, I felt con-nected to The Champ, because if not for his example, I don't believe I would have been confident enough to voice the opin-ion that I had, and then dig my heels in. He taught me, even if subconsciously, that it is of critical importance that we hold a position on the right side of history.

That outlook also influenced my ongoing effort to veer as far as possible from PEDs. I wanted to earn my accomplishments the right way, just like Ali did. He was a Black man who represented Unquestioned Greatness, and that's what I aspired to embody.

Right after I met Ali, I called my father. I was giddy, and given that my admiration of Ali had been passed down to me from my dad, I couldn't wait to share the news with him. Now, as you might have noticed, my father was a hard man to impress. His son being at the Olympics wasn't enough to compel him to come watch my opening heats and qualifying races. This, however, was different, and I had to believe that even he—if only by the slightest degree—would be excited.

I told him what had happened. For a second the line was quiet. "Boy," he said, finally, "I missed that. I should have been there. That's a good man. I should have been there."

Those sentences might as well have been a long letter. I knew what they signified, and so did my father. Like many West Indian men, he wasn't the type to gush to his sons and tell them how proud he was of them. He would speak around it, in a way. And those eighteen words on the phone revealed to me that he was indeed proud of my accomplishments.

I had reached unprecedented heights of athletic achievement over the past two weeks. But impressing my dad by meeting his hero—who knew who *I* was—was an accomplishment that even my two new gold medals didn't compare to.

Nor did my new ring, though I liked it very much. I had bought twelve custom rings for the relay team, coaches and staff—job well done, everyone. And those rings were very big.

CHAPTER 7

UNDISPUTED

COMING OUT OF ATLANTA, I had no reason to believe my gold medal in the 100-metre didn't speak for itself. I was a clean sprinter who had set a world record in the premier event of the Summer Olympic Games. I'd recorded a faster time than anyone in the history of the world. I owned the title of the World's Fastest Man. My status was as cut and dry as it gets. Or so it should have been.

It turned out that Bob Costas, the iconic American broadcaster, believed otherwise. And as the events played out, his words presented a career-altering scenario for me.

Costas was working as host of the 1996 Olympics for NBC and was on the air the night U.S. sprinter Michael Johnson broke the world record in the 200-metre event with a time of 19.32 seconds. Maybe you can see where I'm going with this. Bob proclaimed that if you divided Michael's gold-medal result in that race by two, you would get a time of 9.66 in 100 metres. That, he argued, made Michael a faster man than me, because I had posted a time of just 9.84 in the 100.

Many people were tuned into the NBC broadcast and heard Bob say that. Some even believed him. I have no problems with the man, because I know that, in the end, he was just doing his job. NBC needed an American hero at the Olympic Games taking place on their home soil, and Michael was the man. His impressive accomplishments—winning the gold in both the 200- and 400-metre races—created a space for them to declare that it was him, in fact, who should own the title of World's Fastest Man.

The math seemed seductively simple, but it simply didn't add up. At the time I remarked that Costas "knew nothing about track." That might have been harsh in its phrasing, but we were all clearly in the business of stirring up trouble, and I was happy to play my part. That said, I still stand by the sentiment behind it. Any track and field aficionado would have heard the calculation Costas was selling to the American public and realized it was totally flawed.

When you sprint the 100-metre, you spend almost one-third of the distance gathering speed. It's a few seconds of acceleration until you reach top flight, and once you get there, it's a short distance before the competition is over. In the 200-metre event, the second half does not include an acceleration phase. You have what's called a "flying start."

The 100-metre event is more about raw power, while the 200 requires enduring speed. The former is a Formula One race, while the latter is NASCAR. When Michael did run 100-metre races over the course of his career, he could not break the ten-second mark. He had zero chance of doing that. He was not strong enough and had instead trained his body for efficiency and endurance.

If you look at Bob's calculations for Michael (9.66/100 metres) and then at my result (9.84/100 metres), you will see a massive gap. A 0.18-second difference might not seem like much to people outside of the track and field world, but when you value milliseconds like we do, that gap is astronomical. It would be like a soccer team beating their opponent thirty to zero—in the first half.

Now, did anybody in the world think that Michael Johnson could beat me by that type of margin? Of course not. Bob's claim just didn't make sense. If you doubt me, then maybe ask yourself why he wasn't on the track in Atlanta with me, Linford Christie, Frankie Fredericks and the others. Consider too, during the 100-metre final I'd achieved a top speed of 12.1 metres per second, or 43.6 kilometres an hour. That was the fastest recorded speed of a human runner in history. If I ran that fast down your neighbourhood street, I'd be speeding. Argue with that math. And if none of that convinces you, then try adding my relay time of 8.5, with its flying start, to my 100-metre time of 9.84. According to Costas's math, I'd run an 18.34 200-metre, a full second faster than Johnson's. How absurd does that sound?

But marketing is a hell of a thing. The conversation about who was truly the fastest man in the world began to grow. It was as if Bob had tossed a lit cigarette on the ground and now the whole forest was on fire. With American media hailing Michael as the fastest, Canadians started taking it personally. We've got this thing in my country about being kind of like a younger sibling to the U.S. It becomes a point of conversation when Canadians measure our international sporting achievements— it almost feels like no matter how much we accomplish, we don't seem to get the same respect as Americans.

There is a newspaper in my hometown called *The Oakville Beaver*. It received numerous letters from residents upset with how the Americans were dismissing my victory. The sentiment was being echoed in papers across Canada. The *Beaver*'s publisher, Ian Oliver, decided to take action and actually launched an advertising campaign in the U.S. to promote me as the "World's Fastest Man." He took out ad space in *USA Today* and received more than $7,000 from Canadian supporters to pay for it. I appreciated and respected that. While his support was among the most publicly vocal, there were plenty of people I heard from personally who agreed with Mr. Oliver and were just as enraged as he was.

Inevitably, business folk saw this tug-of-war with Americans over the coveted title and went looking for a way to capitalize on it. And they found one. An Ottawa-based entity called Magellan Entertainment Group approached me and my track agents, Mark Block and Ray Flynn, with the idea of a one-on-one, 150-metre competition between Michael and me, splitting the difference between our two specialties (100-metre and 200-metre). Magellan was a small group that specialized in corporate motivational seminars, and while this may have been of broader scope than their usual events, I thought the idea was good. They proposed a strong hand for Michael and me in controlling how the event would come together, and an appearance fee of U.S.$500,000 for each athlete. The winner would take home an additional $1 million.

In theory, the 150-metre distance provided advantages and disadvantages for each of us. The 100-metre sprinter could fatigue once he'd covered about 70 percent of the distance, and that's where the 200-metre runner could make up ground lost early to his more muscular opponent. Las Vegas bookmakers seemed to side with the 200-metre guy, as evidenced by the three-to-one odds they offered in favour of Michael. I smiled when I saw that. I was going to crush those odds. To my mind, you always bet on the big power guy over the aerobics dude.

The event was going to be the first of its kind in track and field. Best against best, with the winner claiming the title of World's Fastest Man and putting an end to any ambiguity. My team loved the idea and felt it was a no-lose situation. We believed that I would dominate on the track, further vaulting the celebrity I'd won at Atlanta, and if I could do that with an incredible economic opportunity tied in, then why not accept? Michael's team seemed to feel the same way about the upside for him, and he and I both signed on with Magellan.

An important aspect of the event for Michael and I was that it was athlete-driven and athlete-owned. We were essentially the promoters and had our say in planning nearly every element of the race. This put control into our hands, not the hands of national and international sports bureaucracies. We weren't racing in anyone's show; in this case, *we* were the show—and we were getting paid accordingly. Creative control was important to me, and I wanted the competition to happen in Canada. I wanted to bring the highest level of my sport back to my country. Michael had no issues with showing up in Toronto to pick up half a million dollars. Canada hadn't hosted an event of this calibre in twenty-one years, since the 1976 Summer Olympics in Montreal. I viewed this as a chance to perform in front of my people and make them proud, in person. It was my way of thanking them for the incredible support they had given me all throughout 1996.

The initial plans were for a four-competition package. The first event was set for June 1, 1997, at the SkyDome (now called the Rogers Centre) in Toronto, which was home to the Blue Jays of Major League Baseball. It wouldn't have been lost on fans that the Blue Jays had recently won the 1992 and 1993 World Series playing in this stadium, the first MLB championships outside of the United States. There was no place more appropriate to beat the Americans in a sport they traditionally dominated.

The other competitions were supposed to take place in Las Vegas, London and Tokyo. The idea was to bring my great British competitor Linford Christie into the fold along with other athletes who might help draw in crowds. Linford was my predecessor as Olympic 100-metre champion, having won gold in the 1992 Games in Barcelona. So, he seemed like a natural fit.

Being at the forefront during the planning process offered valuable lessons in business, and I was primed to learn from the experience. The stakes were quite high, with millions of dollars on the line, and we would be expected to put together a quality event. Never mind that I actually had to compete in it.

I've never been scared of making decisions, though, and my comfort with betting on myself helped me through the process. From marketing to sponsorship to stadium logistics, I dealt with numerous components that required sustained attention. At one point, I immersed myself in Nielsen TV ratings as we were trying to decide on a broadcaster for the event. My agents pitched in, of course, but I spent a lot of time working out the details.

Michael and I did our part to pump the hype machine. A joint press conference in Toronto took on the feel of a prelude to a heavyweight boxing match. A massive group of television and print reporters had gathered in front of the stage as Michael and I took our seats in front of the microphones.

"First of all, I'm not coming in here expecting to lose to anybody," I said.

"I'm the new star of track and field," said Michael. "So, I'm going to take that title."

Global track and field fans' anticipation was huge, in part because of the ready-made narrative that existed: it was a Little Brother versus Big Brother battle. It was a dynamic you might see in international hockey or soccer, only Michael and I weren't surrounded by teammates. We were just two men representing two countries. Michael was running for big, bad America, the global superpower. Meanwhile, I had Canada and the world on my back. Symbolically, I suppose I was the underdog. But that kind of talk never made sense to me. I was number one, and I was going to settle the discussion, once and for all.

The media in both Canada and the U.S. love this type of stuff and did their part to escalate the rivalry. I remember watching a TV report that mentioned that "Canadians were crushed when steroids cancelled Ben Johnson's claim as World's Fastest Man and would be again were Bailey to lose that label this time around." I thought to myself, *Really? This bullshit again.* Hadn't we finally escaped Ben Johnson's long shadow in Atlanta?

The U.S. media, meanwhile, seemed to be writing me off. I've heard some people say that this competition was a way for the Americans to cheapen my accomplishments in the Atlanta Olympics, and I think that's fair. Like I explained, Bob Costas's math didn't make sense, and there really wasn't a need for an event to decide who was the World's Fastest Man. But I also understood the dynamics at play. The U.S. is an incredibly patriotic country, so it had to hurt them deeply when a guy from the little country up north crashed their party in 1996 and stole the show. Then, seven days later, he and three of his fellows kicked their asses all over again. So, when people even today wonder if I felt the media lessened my accomplishments, I don't flinch. Those kinds of questions were all part of the game. We were selling a rivalry, and a rivalry sells best when everything is at stake.

Business aside, the Bailey-Johnson 150-metre competition was a boon for our sport. It raised the profile of track and field with sports fans, catching the attention of people who typically followed only professional team sports. It was the type of event that would have set social media ablaze if Twitter and Instagram had existed then. To this day, people talk to me about the 150 and say that it was responsible for turning them into track fans. New and long-standing fans caught on to the irresistible competitive element to the event, and as you know by now, whenever the spirit of competition comes knocking, I will answer the door—with ego and pride in full effect. I knew I was going to snatch Michael after I took two steps on that track. Add that irresistible competitive element to all the other benefits to my development as a business person and to our sport in general, and there was no way I could pass it up.

The upcoming race caught the attention of a new friend of mine, one I'd made by sheer coincidence while training in Austin. The governor of Texas, George W. Bush, embraced the idea of a race between Michael and me to see who was really the world's fastest. He invited my team and me to dinner at the governor's mansion in Austin. We were all thrilled to accept. It was one thing to chat with the governor in his sweats at the track; it was another to visit him in his element, a historic home that had stood since before the Civil War.

Governor Bush was enamoured with a certain happenstance in the competition. Michael also trained in Texas, at Baylor University in Waco, where he was under the watchful eye of coach Clyde Hart in one of the world's great incubators of track talent. I can't recall the governor's exact words, but he joked that the SkyDome matchup wasn't going to determine the fastest man in the world, but the fastest man in Texas.

Michael and I actually had a good relationship leading into 1997. At one point, several years before, he had even approached me about training with him, saying, "Donovan, if you came in with me, you'd run [the 100] in 9.6 [seconds]." I took that as a kind gesture of respect from him, because he kept a very tight circle at Baylor and trained with only a few people. I didn't need to follow Michael's example to win, evidently, though I might have bought myself some peace of mind had I taken note of how serious he was about keeping his training circle small. But that's a story for later.

With so much at stake, and the demands of the spectacle taking over, tensions rose as the 150 race grew near. I began to view Michael in the same way a boxer would look at his opponent. Him simply opening his mouth was enough to piss me off.

We sniped at each other during our interviews with the media. Every now and then, I'd hear his quotes, and I'd fire back during my next press availability. Maybe it was all mind games from his perspective, but here's the thing: I understood Michael and his strengths. He could eviscerate his opponents in the 400 metres because they have a lot of time to think during that race. And he'd probably do the same thing with Ato Boldon and Frankie Fredericks and a couple of guys he ran with in the 200 metres. You see, Michael had established himself as a speed-endurance superstar, and his standing in that realm was well-earned. It intimidated people to the point where he would not only be in their heads before races, but *during*. Even if someone was ahead of Michael in the 400-metre, he knew that no lead was truly safe—*Oh shit, I can hear his footsteps coming behind me.*

The 100 was just a different animal. I was a different animal, too. On a shorter track, even the 150, he simply wasn't in my league. In this jungle, there was less margin for error than what he was used to. One tiny misstep on the track will knock you out.

My aggravation with Michael soon took a back seat to my aggravation with the Magellan team. The final days leading up to the event were among the most stressful in my career. Issues were popping up constantly, and the organizers didn't seem to understand the requirements of a track and field event or even how to manage an event of this magnitude. Their handling of finances and the track layout were particularly frustrating to me. I'll get to that. But basically they were out of their depth. So, my team and I got really hands-on with it. This was in addition to my training, and I really didn't need any distractions. The race was mine if I prepared properly. But I was starting to question whether the demands of organizing it were critically undermining my training. I use the example of a rock band that would play a concert at SkyDome, the Rolling Stones, say. Is their lead singer, Mick Jagger, dealing with the granular details of the stage show as the band is warming up backstage? Probably not. He's going through his vocal exercises and getting into his zone to perform. Not me. Behind the scenes, we were completely out of tune.

First off, Magellan ran into financial issues, and a local businessman, Edwin Cogan, had to step in to provide a bailout of more than $1 million so that Michael and I could get paid. Then there was the track itself. Because of the dimensions of SkyDome, which was primarily used for baseball, it was not possible to build a straight 150-metre track. So there had to be some sort of curve in it. I had wanted a 50-metre curve and a 100-metre straightaway. But when I showed up on the Friday ahead of Sunday's competition, I learned that it had been built with a seventy-five/seventy-five split and a corner that was way too tight. It was not the configuration I had signed up for or the one I had been practising with. Dan believed there was a real chance of injury if I were to sprint on a track that curved that tightly. The bend was so sharp that I'd have to alter my gait and potentially introduce a change—at full speed—that my body had not been trained to expect or handle. I asked for the straightaway to be extended and was told by Magellan that it was not possible because that would cut into the space needed for seating and television cameras.

As I'd tried to make my former agent understand, when athletes are the attraction, the requirements for their peak performance come first. The demands of media and audience seating can't take over, because the cameras wouldn't be lined up in rows and the seats wouldn't be sold out if anyone thought the sprinters wouldn't be in top form. It's simple—in theory. It gets turned around very easily when there's a lot of money involved.

Dan asked me how I thought we should handle the sharp turn. My starting blocks were a few metres behind Michael's, and he was on the outside. "Well, I'm bigger, faster and more powerful than him, so I will catch him on the inside," I told Dan. "I will catch him, and before we enter the turn, I will already be up."

I was maybe twenty-five pounds heavier than Michael. I'd won silver in the national championships racing the 200 back in 1993, but since then Dan had bulked me up to specialize in the 100. I knew that the muscle that let me explode on the shorter track would eventually weigh me down over a longer sprint. But I was very confident that 150 metres wouldn't be long enough for Michael to exploit that advantage.

Still, I was deeply aggravated: I was in the best shape of my career and about to deliver a major-league spectacle for my home fans, but I was risking injury by stepping onto that track. I didn't forfeit, obviously, but I went home that weekend with a lot more than winning on my mind.

I had to get all the stress off my chest. Dan had taught me to lose the baggage before I showed up at the track. I was a restless blend of frustration and worry, even though I knew I'd kick Michael's ass.

Usually, ahead of major events, I would stick with my routine and go to bed early. There wasn't a chance of that now. I called my girlfriend over. Saturday night went late.

When I got to SkyDome on Sunday, I still wasn't settled. In today's sporting landscape, a star athlete like LeBron James would be able to voice his displeasure about something like court conditions with a simple tweet and move on. End of story. That wasn't available in 1997, but a press release was, and so I used one to say my piece. I issued a written statement just before the event on Sunday, letting the world know that I was "running under mental duress." And with that, I had to let it go. It was time to run or forfeit, and as the stadium filled with a raucous crowd mostly wrapped in Canadian colours, forfeiting was not an option.

Once I stepped onto the SkyDome floor, all the talk about the curvature of the track left my mind. As I walked toward my starting blocks, years of practice and competition took over my nerves and I entered my internal zone. By the time I crouched into the blocks, it felt to me like there was nobody in the stadium. Later, when I watched video of the race, I was surprised at how loud the stadium actually was. Usually, a crowd will become still before the starting pistol fires and many people will hold their breath until someone crosses the finish line. In Toronto, the fans never stopped cheering. It was a party for the

30,000 people in attendance, which included pretty much every single person I'd grown up with and become friends with during my life. With no heats or qualifying races before the main event, even my father was there cheering me on.

There were also 600 media members covering the event and 2.5 million people watching the CBC's live broadcast. Somebody mentioned to me later that it had the feel of a heavyweight bout. The United States versus Canada. On our soil.

There were no false starts in this competition. Once the gun sounded, I did exactly what I told Dan I would do. I caught Michael within the first ten metres and began to really distance myself from him. Once the track straightened, it was all but over. I finished with a time of 14.99 seconds. Just before I crossed the line, I looked back to see where Michael was. I didn't hear or feel him on my back and wondered what was happening.

When I realized, even before I had crossed the line, that Michael had pulled up at around the 100-metre mark with what I later heard was a hamstring injury (or a quad injury, or a cramp—I heard them all), I thought, "Here we go again." In a swarm of journalists and cameramen a few minutes after the competition, I said in an interview with CBC that Michael "didn't pull up. He's a chicken. He didn't pull up at all. He's just a chicken. He's afraid to lose. I think what we should do is run this race over again, so I can kick his ass one more time."

While that was said in the heat of the moment, I didn't walk it back then and I won't now. At the end of the race, I had continued right up to the vertical mats, placed there to stop athletes with excess momentum, and even took a stride up them before spinning around and dropping back to the track. I howled in that moment. I might have looked triumphant, but I'll tell you right now it wasn't all good feelings. A lot of frustration was fuelling that scream, too. The Olympic champion, world champion and 100-metre world-record holder—doubted publicly by the US media. The long shadow of Ben Johnson and all the trouble I'd taken to stay clean—and I was undeniably drug-free. The Toronto race should never have been needed to claim the title of World's Fastest Man, but I'd embraced the event as an opportunity for our sport, and the result should have been unquestionable. Michael was already well behind me when he'd pulled up. He was never going to beat me on anything shorter than 200 metres, and I'd worked myself into the best race condition of my life to make sure there could be zero doubt at the finish line. And yet, here I was at the end of the track, victorious, and the only thing louder than the roar of the crowd was the excuses I could already hear: Michael was hurt, it doesn't count.

In the end, the media was too flustered by my "chicken" comment to debate the race result. Canadian journalist James Christie said that I "lowered [my] standard to the Americans," while Stephen Brunt wrote, "When he crossed the finish line at the SkyDome, Johnson having pulled up lame, it was an occasion for one of those rare surges of patriotic emotion from a people not prone to let it all hang out. Not quite Paul Henderson. Not quite Ben before the fall. But close enough to do the trick . . . And then, with the flags waving, with the anthem playing, Bailey had to go and act, well, so un-Canadian."

I walked away from my victory against Michael with a feeling of emptiness. It would have been much more satisfying if he had put up a fight. Over the next few days, I did some television spots to capitalize on the attention received by the event, and on a national morning show apologized for what I'd said about Michael. But the words were barely out of my mouth when I was having second thoughts. What was I apologizing for? The language was hardly foul. Chicken? And even in 1997, if you listened to any sports broadcast closely enough, you'd hear a lot worse than "kick his ass" coming from the ice or court or whatever your favourite sport is played on. Michael could take it. He was an accomplished competitor at the peak of his own career. He had won two individual gold medals (200- and 400-metre) in Atlanta, and throughout his career, he would win two more along with seven world championships. His nickname was Superman, and that's who I wanted to beat. Not the guy who quits the race two-thirds of the way to the finish line.

I also had the rematch in mind. SkyDome was supposed to be just the first event in a series, with Vegas up next. Think of Apollo Creed in the *Rocky* film franchise talking up the rematch (a franchise created to erase my hero, the greatest boxer of all time, with Rocky Balboa, the white boxer). Boxing has always been close to my heart, so I know how powerful the idea of The Rematch can be. Nobody can resist it, not fans, not media, not advertisers and certainly not athletes. The reality is that rematches between Michael and me would have fetched us tens of millions of dollars. After sponsor bonuses, I'd cleared $5 million that day, the largest single-day earning in the world history of track and field—a record that will never be broken, I guarantee it. But those earnings from the Toronto event would have paled in comparison to what we could do with the rematches.

Minutes after the race was as good a time as any to start warming up the crowd for round two.

So I was hoping Michael would respond to my comments with fire of his own, something akin to, *Okay, fuck you. I'm going to train and destroy you in our next race.* That's how the 100-metre guys operated. But he stayed mostly silent. My team spoke to his several times about setting up the second competition, and they kept hearing back that Michael was not going to do it. So, the Vegas event didn't happen. Without Michael, there would be none of the heat that had made Toronto so exciting. I dropped the idea of Vegas and went ahead with the competition in London. Linford joined me for that. Then later, in Tokyo, I turned the event into a 100-metre competition. I won both.

I quickly stopped caring about what the media said. I had fulfilled the hopes of Canadian and global track fans, whom I'd made proud in Atlanta and then again here in Toronto. Was reclaiming pride for my country in a nationally televised race that came on the heels of Olympic history considered un-Canadian? Hell, many Canadians have expressed to me over the years that it was their *all-time favourite sporting moment.* They had grown sick and tired of being regarded as distant seconds to the Americans, and this competition allowed a Canadian to reverse the narrative and stand up to the bully.

Despite my frustration, the entire experience felt like a major positive in my track and field career, and it had other longer-lasting benefits. It exposed me to elements of the business world at a scale I had never seen from the inside. I worked closely with advertisers and sponsors and learned a great deal about finance and the inner workings of multi-million-dollar deals. It played a key role in my later graduation from Donovan the athlete to Mr. Bailey the businessman. I've always revered athletes like Michael Jordan and Magic Johnson, who were able to thrive in the upper echelon of both their sport and the boardroom. They weren't defined entirely by their success in a sport. Basketball was only one aspect of their life, and though they could have retired into lives of leisure, resting on their well-earned millions, they went on to accept new challenges, expose themselves to new risks and win again.

The Bailey-Johnson 150-metre event was a one-of-a-kind in the track and field world then and really hasn't been replicated since. Credit goes to Michael for being my partner in breaking that new ground. He understood the gravity of what we were doing, taking our competition beyond the Olympics and world championships, and putting the control, earnings and even the identity of our sport into the hands of athletes themselves.

As successful as the race was, there were consequences—dire consequences I thought I'd dodged. Maybe I should have stuck to my guns about that SkyDome track. Or maybe it was just my time.

CHAPTER 8

RUPTURES AND REGRETS

I DON'T PARTICIPATE.

In August 1997, a mere two months after my competition with Michael in Toronto, I won the silver medal at the world championships in Athens, Greece, with a time of 9.91 seconds. That was .05 seconds behind American gold medallist Maurice Greene. I ran a perfectly executed race in the semi-finals, but didn't transition properly through the finals. I drove through the entire 100 metres, which you don't do. Maurice ran a great race.

I had won a number of meets since the SkyDome race, in Moscow, Nuremberg, Paris and then the Canadian trials in Abbotsford, British Columbia. But I'd dropped to third in Lausanne, and on Canada Day no less. Now I had a participation medal at the worlds. Too many things were weighing on my mind and body, and I was feeling an urgent need to take control of my situation to set them straight.

It was clear to me now that the stress of organizing the SkyDome race had drained me in ways I hadn't anticipated. I felt physically worn down, and my body didn't seem to be recovering as quickly as it had in the past. Toronto had left me with a micro-tear in my abductor muscle, which we could not tell anyone. I'd also lost twelve pounds, which was far more than I'd usually drop during the season. But something else—or someone else—was distracting me in Greece, and he had been hanging around for a while.

We had a coach, Andy McInnis, who had a reputation among the athletes. He showed up at the track in Athens one day on a shining Harley Davidson, posing for pictures with it parked on the track. The athletes had trouble finding the Harley as cool as he did when we realized we had no transportation to and from the track every day while our coach tore around the ancient Greek capital on his flashy ride. The place we were staying didn't have air conditioning, the windows were unfinished and the food was terrible. And the reigning Olympic champion, who didn't have a proper bed to sleep in, was left asking people for a ride back to his lousy accommodations at the end of practice. The team was being run disastrously.

I tore into him. If he was paying more attention to what he was hired to do, we would be better prepared to compete. McInnis survived my criticism, but he couldn't survive his own behaviour. He had been a coach at the Ottawa Lions Track and Field Club since Glenroy had run there as a teenager and Mark Lindsay had been part of their physio team (before Glenroy introduced us). Decades later, in 2020, the club fired McInnis following allegations by female athletes of sexual harassment. The coach appealed his suspension by Athletics Canada but lost. The national team upheld his lifetime ban from the sport. It turned out that the most recent allegations hadn't been his first.

No shit.

I did lead the Canadian men's 4x100-metre relay team to a gold medal with a time of 37.86 seconds. We had beaten the previously unbeatable Americans in Atlanta, and now we'd beaten them in Greece. I'd even bought a $5 million insurance policy that would pay out if the relay team broke the world record. I told Athletics Canada we should do it, because I was the only sprinter making real money. They refused, so I bought a policy myself for the team from Lords of London. We fell a little short, but that didn't change the fact that this was the greatest team in the history of Canadian sport. Something else was bothering me, though. Individually, I was the Olympic champion and world-record holder, and I could not accept silver at the world championships. No way. I could shrug off the irresponsible Canadian coach, but I couldn't accept the suboptimal conditions of my own training. When the professional season was over and I headed back to Austin in September, I had to get serious about an uncomfortable situation.

While training at the University of Texas in preparation for the summer season and the 150-metre event, Dan had been simultaneously working with about thirty other athletes, and they ranged in experience from professionals to amateurs and weekend warriors. I was the only athlete paying Dan, and I didn't appreciate having to line up behind anyone for his time.

Dan was a fair coach. I was his star athlete, but he divided his time equally among his pupils. I respected that. He was showing these athletes the same grace he had showed me when I had needed his fine tuning to take me to the ultimate level. I'd expressed my concerns to him, but he held fast to his open-door approach. This was his side hustle, after all. He was training these athletes on the side, in addition to his university teaching and coaching.

A few days after the final in Greece, I became too sick to race in the final at a meet in Zurich. Later in August, I won Diamond League races in London and Cologne, and took second in Berlin and again in my last race of the summer, Tokyo on September 6. When I returned to Austin to begin fall training, I found Dan's collection of strays had grown even larger.

At the campus one morning, I went for a walk with Dan around the track and told him I needed changes, starting with a separation in our training groups. I wanted him to train the elite athletes in one group and people of other skill levels in another. Dan's own advice had been to "clean out my closet" if I wanted to prepare myself for success. Well, my closet was crowded with a bunch of sprinters I didn't know and couldn't trust, and as a result practices had become the biggest source of my stress.

Let me explain that point. Sharing my coach's time was only one concern. The Ben Johnson scandal had sent the wrong message to some athletes. Ben getting caught and losing his gold medal might have scared off some sensible people from using PEDs. But just as many athletes seemed to have learned from his example that PEDs worked. Steroids and other drugs were everywhere. I'm a suspicious person, and now that I was surrounded every day by so many amateurs and strangers, I grew downright paranoid. Stories were circulating about water bottles getting spiked, and I did not want to put myself even remotely close to a position where that could happen. While at the track, I ate only what food Mark brought with him. I kept my water in sight at all times. The constant worries were clouding my focus.

It had come to a head when we learned that a young Canadian athlete Dan had been training tested positive for steroids. I'd seen the kid watching us from the stands. That was fine, lots of people did that. But then one day he was on the track, training as a member of my group. And now he'd been busted for PEDs. If word got around, I could see the headlines flash across my mind: *Man in Donovan Bailey's training group tests positive for PEDs.*

Dan listened as we paced the track, and I stated my case to him in full. I was matter-of-fact and businesslike about it. I had no need to rant. I'd expressed my concerns to him before, and I knew I'd either get the results I needed or I'd take matters into my own hands.

Stoic as ever, he chewed his tobacco and listened, and the expression on his face never changed.

"You know, Donovan, I gave you a shot and you made good," he said, after hearing me out. "So, some of these people are looking for help. Some of them will never make it anywhere, but I've got to give them a shot."

"Yes, Dan, I understand that," I replied. "But now you and I own the industry. It's now 100 percent business. Let me again reiterate that I'm the only one paying you for your services. So, I'm paying you to coach these people, and I don't know half of them, and 99 percent of them will never make it professionally."

Dan remained steadfast. The amateurs weren't going anywhere. Deep in my heart, I adored that about the man. He would teach and train for nothing and sleep outside in the pole vault pit if he had to. That's what made him an incredible coach, and it's why I respected his stance—no one could ever call him a hypocrite. But I couldn't live with his decision. I could not train with the necessary peace of mind in that chaotic environment. I had too much to lose and, like any elite athlete, only a few short years to make the most of my peak abilities.

"Okay, then, I probably need to go, Dan," I told him. "Who do you recommend as a coach going forward?"

With that we were done. I felt something terrible in the pit of my stomach. Team Bailey was falling apart just as we had ascended to the height of our profession. I was leaving the man who had guided me to such magnificent heights. Dan was a mentor who had connected with me on a cerebral level and cared enough to develop a deep understanding of what made me tick. He'd made the effort to use that knowledge to push me on the track and motivate me to push myself even harder.

In many ways, this disagreement closely resembled the situation with my dad many years ago when I told him I was leaving the business world to pursue track and field. My father was upset then just as Dan was upset now, even though he wouldn't admit it. I was devastated, but as a man who needed to make and live with his own decisions, I needed to go.

Dan recommended I train with a coach named Loren Seagrave, who was based in Atlanta. Within a week, I put my house in Austin up for sale, flew to Atlanta, bought a place there and began training with Loren. I went to Georgia with an open mind, but after just three weeks, I knew Loren and I were not a good fit. I think he knew that as well, and he even remarked a few times, "We see things differently."

Here's the thing: Either you fit with your coach or you don't. With Loren, I didn't. And I quickly realized that he had a very different attitude from Dan when it came to getting paid. Even out on the track, his conversations with me always led to the question of when he was going to receive his money. That was no way to begin our relationship. It was jarring, because it caused me to wonder about his intentions. Was he going to be able to focus and dive deeply into my sprinting mechanics with money at the front of his mind? Dan and I had never even discussed a salary, and yet he was the best-paid track coach every year, enough so that he was able to buy a house.

Money issues aside, Loren was a knowledgeable coach, but he wasn't challenging me, and soon he was telling me what he must have thought I wanted to hear. Everything was, "Yes, Donovan," "Good job, Donovan," "You did it right, Donovan," "That's pretty good, Donovan."

That last one got me riled up. *Pretty good?* I remember thinking. *Nothing is pretty good enough for me. Pretty good to me means that I ran 100 metres in eight seconds flat. We're not there.*

I questioned his coaching technique at times, and I'm sure he did not like that. Whereas Dan would provide detailed answers to the questions I posed, Loren did not. Dating back to my childhood, when I was the "why kid" in Jamaica, I had always had an innate need to gain a deep understanding of whatever I was doing.

Starting off the blocks was the one area of my game that the whole world knew I needed to improve on. I tended to keep my hips too high during my starting position, and that resulted in my first step being too high as well. My scoliosis probably contributed to that. The posture wasn't efficient, and my first steps were often in a zigzag pattern before my trajectory straightened out. Loren tried his hand at improving that, and we lingered there during our training. His idea was to overhaul my mechanics, whereas Dan had been more of a tweaker. Loren worked on changing how my front foot would contact the ground, and he also had me try different shin angles. Upon reflection, if I had been in a better headspace, maybe I would have got a lot more out of those adjustments. But I think the frustration of parting with Dan, someone I trusted 1,000 percent, might have been causing me to throw up a level of resistance with Loren.

I didn't want to be in Atlanta.

My mind often wandered back to Austin, and I'd reminisce. I was a creature of habit, and Dan and I had our thing that worked, a rapport that was forged in the fire, so to speak. Gruff and plain-spoken as he was, we could be vulnerable with each other in our own way. What I missed the most was the non-verbal communication between us—or at least the communication with the fewest words possible.

Sitting by the track one day in Atlanta, I thought back to the 1995 world championships in Gothenburg, Sweden. Dan was walking me to the call room, where all the athletes gathered before a competition. When we arrived at the door, he gave me an expressionless look and said, "Well, I've done all that I can do. Let's see what you got." I let out a hearty laugh and responded, "That's the big speech?" We were so in sync that I didn't need platitudes from Dan. We were travelling on the same deep frequency. Good times.

I thought about calling him. I couldn't. Sure, I was the one who had walked away, but to me, the decision had been mutual. I'd needed things to change, and he'd held his ground. I was hurting, and my pride didn't allow me to ask for his help. As it turned out, I didn't need to ask—I didn't have to ask Dan, that is. My long-time medical point person, the chiropractor Dr. Mark Lindsay, had come to Atlanta to work with me. He and Dan were speaking every day about other athletes in their mutual care. They had a strong relationship of their own. Soon enough, in almost comedic fashion, Mark became a middleman between Dan and me.

When chatting with Mark, Dan would ask him how practice was going with me. Mark would answer, and then Dan would casually slip in some information about the latest sprinting workout he had devised, knowing that Mark would soon be speaking to me. Mark would approach me the next day with a new workout that he figured I could incorporate into my training with Loren. I did so knowing full well where that suggestion had come from. It was funny; Dan and I were too proud to speak with each other, and yet here we were communicating through Mark. We were very stubborn men. We were like a father and son who were mad at each other but were still calling home frequently to ask our wife/mom how the other person was faring.

I blinked first. One day, while chatting with Mark, I asked him, "Have you spoken with Dan?"

"Of course," he responded. "He gave me this feedback for you."

From then on, it was out in the open. Dan was essentially coaching me from a distance. Sure, it may have been different and felt a bit strange at first. But ultimately, when it comes to family, there's a sense of home that shines through. And Dan was and still is family to me.

The summer of 1998 wasn't so much my triumphant return to the track as it was evidence that I wasn't where I belonged. The Goodwill Games in New York City in late July were the best example of that.

Just like the Olympics, which these games were meant to emulate, the 100-metre would be the centrepiece. It was my return to a big stage in the U.S., and with Maurice Greene winning the world championship in Greece, the games when our coach was enjoying his Harley Davidson more than his job, the final was hyped as a showdown between the Americans, keen to reassert their dominance in the sport, and the world, represented by the reigning Olympic champion and world-record holder.

I'd had eight podium finishes in a row leading up to the competition, but I didn't feel good. I felt injury prone and, given the enormity of the event, ill-prepared. I was accustomed to going over all my contingency plans with Dan before competitions—what to do if it was windy, or raining, or if I got off to a bad start. I was feeling physically and psychologically drained. I'd rather have been at home. The level of readiness that always gave me comfort and allowed me to optimize my focus wasn't there.

In the final, my start was terrible. My starts were often weak, but this one was as bad as my starts get. Only thirty or forty metres in, I shut it down. I knew I could beat Greene, but I didn't have it together that day. Two weeks after that, I competed in Zurich, re-injuring my quad, and ended my season. I moved out of my place in Atlanta and went home to Oakville. I needed to spend some time in touch with my roots. I settled in for a summer and fall chilling with my friends and family and getting ready for my big brother O'Neil's wedding.

A time that should have been about finding peace very soon turned into something painfully different.

As much as I'd forever attached my name to sprinting history, I'd still rather have been running up and down a hardwood court.

Even during the apex of my sprinting career, there were days I would tune into NBA games and wish I had had the opportunity to pursue a life in basketball. I followed each season closely and kept track of all the star players in the league. When the Toronto Raptors came into existence in 1995 (alongside the short-lived Vancouver Grizzlies), it gave Canadians a team to rally behind. Though I was rarely in the city at that time, I did try to make the odd game. To this day, I'm good friends with Isiah Thomas, the legendary Detroit Pistons point guard who became the Raptors' inaugural general manager, and the original team owners, the Bitove family.

I had friends coaching the Ontario under-nineteen team, and one day in September, they called me up. They were getting a couple of the fellows together for a pickup game at Sheridan College. That was *my* gym, where I had wowed people with my athleticism during my year there. My pals were offering me the chance to play ball again at my old stomping grounds, and you can best believe I wasn't going to turn that down.

By this time, I could go through my extensive warm-up routine with hardly thinking about it. But that was for sprinting. I didn't feel the need to stretch and activate before a basketball game with friends. In school I had warmed up *during* the game. A few jogs up and down the court on offence and defence were enough to get the blood flowing.

Early on in the game, I was playing defence when I felt something off in my left leg. A moment earlier, I'd made a play that left my feet in an awkward position, so I thought nothing more of the discomfort. I was having a really good game and wanted to keep up the momentum. The whistle blew for a stoppage, and I was simply walking backwards, as slow as you can imagine, when I heard a pop. My body had never made that sound, almost like a shot from a pistol with a silencer attached. At first, I didn't realize that it had come from me. But when I looked down, the reality was stark.

I tried to lift my foot, but as hard as I tried, I could not raise my toe from the hardwood. When I saw my foot flopping, my stomach dropped. You see injuries around the track, and you learn to recognize the signs and symptoms of a body in trouble.

Mark Witherspoon, an American sprinter, had once described hearing the same gunshot sound during the 100-metre semi-final at the 1992 Barcelona Olympics.

That gut-wrenching little sound was the tearing of my Achilles tendon.

This was bad.

Complicating the gravity of the moment was the presence of several local media members in the gym. They had heard I was going to be appearing for a game of pickup and showed up for a story. I had to keep it together.

I called out to my friend and teammate Ron and waved him over. I told him I had a cramp in my calf and was done for the day.

He looked at me and said, "What the fuck are you talking about?"

"Don't worry about it," I said, trying to keep a surge of emotion from becoming noticeable. "Give me your shoulder so I can walk off."

As Ron helped me off the court, I smiled and waved to the members of the press.

"Guys, listen, I have a cramp. I gotta go."

I didn't want the media creating a ruckus and sought to keep the injury on the down-low. Ron helped me into the locker room, where I grabbed my knapsack and hopped to my car. I told Ron not to worry about me, to go back inside and have fun. I'd be fine. Meanwhile, I knew that I needed to drive myself to the hospital immediately. Thankfully, my right leg was fine, so I was able to operate my car.

As I drove toward Oakville Trafalgar Memorial Hospital, all kinds of thoughts rattled around in my head. I had suffered injuries on the track before, such as a pulled hamstring and an upper thigh tear, and I understood that the human body doesn't necessarily warn you when something is amiss. It doesn't know that you're going to be extending a muscle or tendon to the degree that you do when participating in rigorous activity, and so oftentimes the injury seems to appear out of nowhere. Like a thief in the night.

My body had been stressed for months. Loren was coaching me to use techniques and movements that were new to me. Even though I had had only a few months' worth of real work with him, Loren had really tried to tweak my starts, utilizing a method that I believe placed unfamiliar stress on my back, hips, quads, hamstrings and Achilles.

As I reached a traffic light and put on the brakes, a thought popped in my head that made me want to vomit. *If I stayed with Dan, would I even be in this situation?*

Let me just tell you: that kind of regret can haunt an athlete for their whole life.

When I reached the emergency ward, I called Mark, who happened to be driving with his wife, Kate, on the QEW near Toronto, about half an hour away. With all that restrained emotion now pouring out, I described what had happened. I was so rattled and upset by this point that after I hung up I just left my Mercedes S600 sitting in front of the emergency doors as if it were valet parking at a nightclub. I asked a gentleman at the door who recognized me if he could get me a wheelchair and then proceeded to roll myself to triage. Somebody took my keys later on and parked my car.

I underwent tests on my leg, and eventually the surgeon, Dr. Deakon, walked into the room and looked at me lying in pain on the hospital bed. I told him, "Let's fix this. I've got a lot of work ahead of me."

"Hey, man," he said, "I don't know if my career can handle this. You're the fastest human on the planet, and you've got a ruptured Achilles." Dr. Deakon wasn't being flippant. He was simply emphasizing how bad he felt delivering potentially career-ending news to me.

I clearly didn't understand the need for that kind of sympathy.

My Achilles was not simply torn; the tendon had completely shredded. My calf muscle was rolled up like a dinner roll below the back of my knee. When Mark and Kate arrived at the hospital and learned of the diagnosis, Kate, a former world-champion and Olympic alpine skier, burst into tears. She had blown out her knee years ago and was never the same athlete again. In her mind, my career was over. Mark began to cry as well.

Mark and Kate knew all about injuries, and seeing them that concerned, I probably should have been terrified. I wasn't though. I absorbed their emotion and deeply appreciated it. But I didn't cry. In my head, I was still invincible, and this was simply another challenge to overcome. It was a big one, sure, but I had come back from injuries before. Why should this one be any different?

There are times when my bravado gets me into trouble and people can deem it as arrogance. But in this instance, that bravado was exactly what I needed. I didn't understand the severity of the injury or how hard the rehab was going to be. My attitude probably saved my career.

The media caught wind of my injury, and it was soon all over the news. We had the TV on in my room, and I was flipping the channels when I came across a report about me. A journalist was interviewing Dr. Michael Clarfield, the Toronto Maple Leafs' team physician. If my bravado was bubbling before I saw him, it had exploded into hot lava by the time he finished speaking.

"Donovan," Clarfield proclaimed, "will never be able to run again."

I sat up in my bed and squeezed the remote so hard I nearly broke it.

"He might not even be able to walk properly."

I can't describe to you the anger that began to course through my veins. "Fuck that!" I yelled. "I'm going to show you something."

Looking back, in a calmer state of mind, I respect and value the opinions of professionals. But in the heat of the moment, I was severely irritated hearing someone who didn't know me saying that I would never be a world-class sprinter again. Right then, I decided to treat my recovery as if Dr. Clarfield had just issued me a direct challenge. He might as well have been Michael Johnson or Frankie Fredericks. I was going to shove that prediction right up his ass—with my left foot. *A guy's never come back from surgery and become the fastest man in the world? Watch me.*

CHAPTER 9

RACING FATHER TIME

WHENEVER I HAVE a clearly identified goal, the effort that goes into accomplishing it becomes easier.

When I first settled on the target of becoming a successful sprinter, the steps that I needed to take to make it happen didn't feel laborious. I left my career in Canada behind and moved to Louisiana. Sure, there were sacrifices that had to be made and time that had to be devoted to my craft. But I woke up every morning looking forward to the day ahead and making some sort of progress, even if it was incremental, toward my goal.

I decided to approach the rehab from my Achilles injury with the same mindset. Mark and I had a serious discussion about whether I should retire. But as the doctor had pointed out, I was the fastest human alive. I was going to compete again. And I was going to win.

My surgery was performed by Dr. Anthony Miniaci of the Cleveland Clinic, a renowned orthopedic surgeon who had been on staff with the Cleveland Browns of the National Football League and consulted with the Toronto Blue Jays, among many other professional sports organizations. I was on the operating table within a day of suffering the injury and, thankfully, underwent a successful procedure. My Achilles had been so tight that, when it popped, it tore into little spaghetti-like strands. Dr. Miniaci had to weave them together like hair and then attach the end to one little nub of my ankle.

The regular protocol for recovery from this type of operation required me to wear a cast for six to eight weeks following the knife, and only then would rehab begin. But Mark and I determined that, in order to expedite my complete recovery, we needed to do things differently. I was fitted with a removable cast, and as soon as the wound on my skin had fully healed—in four days—Mark removed the cast to work on my Achilles and the area around it. He began with a daily intensive, hands-on therapy called "stripping," which meant pressing his thumbs with force up and down the newly reattached Achilles to break up the scar tissue as quickly as it could form. It was the most intense physical pain I've ever endured. I say that without hyperbole. It felt like 1,000 hot needles stabbing me with full force. Just thinking about it gives me goosebumps, but I knew that we had to make sure that my Achilles was as strong and flexible as before the injury. Its elasticity was vitally important if I was to regain my peak speed on the track.

I always felt that Mark had holy hands. I knew that I could make outrageous demands of my body, and at the end of the day, he would be there to put everything back together. I trusted him implicitly, and there was no one I would have rather had put me through this difficult rehab—much more difficult than the rehab from my quad injury in 1992. I was more grateful than ever for Mark's dedication and expertise, because I quickly learned that muscle injuries are not in the same league as those that involve tendons. This was a whole new level of pain.

As soon as I was able to put a little weight on my leg, Mark sent me with Kate to the pool at Etobicoke Centennial Stadium. We were doing the workouts Dan was recommending to Mark from Austin, but with a life jacket on and my feet not touching the bottom. I was soon regaining strength in my leg. I hit the weight room, too, though initially I was doing my squats and lifts on only one leg. We couldn't allow my good leg to atrophy while waiting for the other to catch up. Nor could we allow the strength of the injured leg to fall too far behind while waiting for the Achilles to heal. So after my pool and weight-room work, Mark would put me on the table and manually break down the muscle in my left leg, simulating the natural muscle damage of lifting weights to keep pace with the right leg. He also employed naturopathic medicine and acupuncture.

I could have made rehab easier on myself by taking painkillers, but I opted not to. In Jamaica, we are raised with a disregard for unnecessary pharmaceuticals. My mom and grandmother had naturopathic and herbal remedies for anything that ailed us, and they never involved a pill. That attitude was bred into me, and now, professionally, I needed always to be wary of drugs. I had seen what happened to other sprinters who didn't take the importance of staying clean seriously enough, and it would be easy enough to ingest a painkiller that I didn't realize was banned. I wasn't going to risk jeopardizing my reputation or future standing. I was well on my way to becoming the most drug-tested athlete in the history of sport, with fifty tests a year during the peak of my career. If steering clear of drugs meant debilitating pain, I would just shift my thoughts toward my goal of competing again and bear it out. There were some days when my Achilles would swell up like a balloon, but I trudged on, with my mind set on future victories.

If I struggled, I thought back to Dr. Clarfield's words, which would frequently flash across my mind like a ticker in Times Square: *Donovan will never be able to run again.* That comment filled me with pure spite. It was my oxycodone.

Dan and I made amends.

I knew our reunion was inevitable. So did Mark. He had told Dan that we needed to quit our bullshit and get back to work. In January 1999, Dan welcomed me with open arms in Texas, and we continued almost right where we left off. There was no awkwardness. We were just like family members at a reunion. There was a quick, almost fatherly hug, but it wasn't like that joyous bear hug I gave him back in 1994 when I arrived at LSU for training. No, this was a quick, non-verbal way to say, *Welcome home. Now let's get back to business.* I was thirty years old and rehabbing an injury that would have threatened the career of even a much younger athlete. A sense of urgency drove me, and Dan didn't need to be told how I was feeling about my future.

The thing that had driven me away from Austin was my concern about training with a large group of strangers. When I got to Austin, I found a small, tight group that answered my prayers and ended my frustrations. All elite sprinters and solid individuals, including Kareem Streete-Thompson, Obadele Thompson, Glenroy. This was the kind of group I could surround myself with and be at peace.

When my Achilles was strong enough to get back on the track, I had a few hiccups. At first, the simple act of running felt quite strange. For years I had trusted that I could just reach inside, turn on a switch and perform at an optimum level. It was different now. I sometimes felt dead spots in my left foot. I had learned over the years to be hyper-aware of how every inch of me felt at all times, and now everything felt different.

If you look at sprinting as if it were music, then it felt like I was skipping a beat. I would step off the track and Dan would tell me that I dropped my front foot at the seventy-metre mark. "You've got to watch that," he told me once. "Because your hip is very high, Donovan. If you collapse on it, you could break your hip and ankle."

I had to restabilize my left and right sides, putting extra weight when lifting on my left while also teaching my legs to sync again. All the technical training I'd absorbed from Dan over the past years—right to the point of walking properly— I had to learn it all over again.

I had spent close to half a dozen years preparing my body for its apex in 1996. Now I was trying to cram in the same amount of preparation in just half a dozen months.

My goal was to compete and win again, so I needed a target. Circling a date on the calendar went a long way to driving me down my road to recovery. And that date was July 23, the opening of the 1999 Pan American Games in Winnipeg.

The Games were to be held less than a year after my injury and only six months after I'd resumed training. The marketing for the games was centred around my participation, and I signed a contract to serve as a paid ambassador. Dan recommended that I pass on the 100-metre and just focus on the relay. That would provide a nice way to re-enter competition without putting the full measure of stress on my Achilles. It went against my nature, but I trusted Dan.

Not everyone wanted to put my recovery first. I took a lot of grief for skipping the 100-metre.

Canadian rower Marnie McBean, who won three Olympic gold medals in team events during her career, was particularly critical, saying that I should give back the $200,000 I was reportedly paid (it was actually a lot more than that) for promoting the Pan Am Games and split it among all Canadian athletes. I never spoke to Marnie about this, but it was common back then for athletes to chirp in the media without actually confronting me. I did everything in my contract to promote the Pan Am Games ahead of the event. In November, for instance, I walked the game ball onto the field during the opening ceremonies of the Grey Cup, Canada's football championship game. I was in the middle of my Achilles rehab and could barely walk, but I fulfilled my obligation. My involvement helped put butts in seats at the Pan Am Games, even if I was competing only in the relay.

Dan was angry that people were questioning me. He later shared his thoughts with Brent McFarlane, a Canadian track and field coach, in the latter's autobiography, *Standing Alone*: "Most people do not realize that if Donovan was a professional football or basketball player, he would not have competed in 1999," Dan said, and he went on to call my comeback "a miracle." Why, he challenged, would anyone who was still nursing a serious injury anchor the relay *and* run the 100-metre in the 1999 Pan Am Games (and later, the world championships in Seville)? It would have been a recipe for undoing all the rehabilitation work I'd done since my injury—and maybe making it worse.

Preparing myself for any role on the relay squad was a massive undertaking. Questioning my commitment to the team and my country, given the steep hill I had to climb, was unfair. I could completely embarrass myself and Canada if I wasn't realistic about what my body could handle at this stage of my recovery.

"Did nobody in Canada see that?" asked Dan. "How many Canadians gave him credit for this accomplishment and remarkable comeback? None! Instead, they were merciless in their criticism of Donovan for not running both the 100m and anchoring the men's 4x100m relay at the Pan Am Games and World Championships."

It was shades of Harry Jerome, the Canadian sprinter who had tied for the 100-metre world record when he was only nineteen. At the Rome Olympics in 1960, Jerome injured his hamstring when leading a 100-metre semifinal. The injury was severe enough that he had to pull up. Media accused him of quitting, and one article bizarrely complained about his "bad manners." Two years later he tore his quadriceps at the British Empire and Commonwealth Games in Perth, Australia. The knives were out again. The criticisms were ignorant, and worse they seemed almost happy to see the young athlete fail. Now here I was, going through a version of the same thing, as the suspiciously injured Black athlete of the day.

I listened to my coach. I didn't pay attention to the things other people were saying about me. Dan and I had made a decision, and I looked at it as just another step in my grand scheme of becoming one of the best in the world again. What I couldn't ignore was Dr. Clarfield's statement. His words kept ringing in my head, and I intended to shove them down the throats of everyone who doubted me.

As Dan advised, I would be the leadoff man on the relay team. Dan felt I would be less likely to reinjure my leg, or cause myself a new injury, if I started my leg of the race coming out of the blocks. This wasn't a decision based on his technical knowledge. Instead, it was based on his knowledge of my personality. Dan felt that if I was the anchor and we were down when the baton got to me, I would rip my Achilles apart in an all-out effort to catch up and win. And even if I didn't reinjure the Achilles, I'd stress it and risk reinjury over the remainder of the season. We were at home in Canada—the hosts of the party. My coach knew who I was and what drove me. I trusted Mark and I trusted Dan, and Dan was trying to save me from myself.

Glenroy was running the second leg, followed by Bradley McCuaig and Trevino Betty. I was very happy with my performance. I handed the baton off to Glenroy, having staked us to a significant lead, and he took care of business, just as he always did in relays. Glenroy's relay success was like clockwork. Trevino struggled to close things out, though, and we finished behind Brazil to capture the silver medal.

I was angry. I knew if I had been the anchor, that wouldn't have happened. Yes, it was gratifying to get out there and compete—I wasn't hesitant or timid with my movements, which Dan and I took as a good sign—but we had just won a participation medal on our home turf. In the moment, I would rather have reruptured my Achilles than settle for silver.

Following that race, Dan and I went back to the elements in my game that needed fine tuning, given that I had been out of action for about nine months. I needed to relearn my gait and cadence and re-establish the power that had propelled me in years past. I'd upheld my leg of the relay, yes, but I hadn't matched my old speed, and anything less was not going to be good enough to repeat as Olympic champion. And that was the goal.

As the 2000 Summer Olympics in Sydney approached, the goal came into clear view. I was determined to become the first repeat 100-metre Olympic champion to cross the line first in both years (Carl Lewis finished second behind Ben Johnson in 1998 before Ben's disqualification gave Carl his second gold). If I could defend my title and represent Canada there, it would check off the box in my head—I would have returned to the status of world-class sprinter.

The difference between Atlanta 1996 and Sydney 2000 was stark to me. In the former, I was climbing up the mountain, and in the latter, I was already perched on its peak. However, in truth, the 2000 Games always felt like a daunting task. I had only just run my first post-surgery sub-ten in the 100-metre in June 2000, when I won the Spitzen Leichtathletik Luzern meet in Lucerne, Switzerland, with a time of 9.98 seconds. That was nearly a year after the Pan Am Games in Winnipeg, and it qualified me for Sydney. It was a special achievement in itself—the same time that had got me through the Canadian Olympic trials in Montreal on my way to Atlanta four years earlier. As the years have passed, I've come to appreciate the number that I posted. People had written me off and said my career was over, but here I was posting a *sub-ten*. There are many sprinters in this world who would sell their soul to have 9.98 seconds represent their career best time. I was doing it on one foot.

At the time, however, I wasn't appreciating anything of the kind. In Australia I would be facing off against healthy competitors such as Maurice Greene and Ato Boldon, while I was still struggling to find a consistent feeling of comfort on the track. My recent competitions had been hit and miss. I had finished first in Switzerland, but there were other events where I ran like shit. Each morning that year, I'd wake up and ask, *Okay, which body is going to show up today?* That was a new and unwelcome feeling.

With my spot in the Olympics secured, my competitive spirit, unlike my body, was still in top form. I wanted to win again on the Olympic stage. The Summer Games come around only once every four years, so with the lingering effects of the injury this would be, in all likelihood, my final Olympics. I would be nearly thirty-seven years old during the 2004 Summer Games in Athens. It isn't impossible to compete at that age, but who knows what injuries I'd suffer in the meantime.

When I arrived in Australia, I was feeling good. After settling in, I went through a few workouts and was gearing up for the preliminary races. One day, while I was being worked on by a therapist, I experienced chills. That was it. Nothing more. Nothing to worry about. I kept my focus on the upcoming heats. Until, that is, I faced a needless distraction from the usual source, the Canadian officials.

As vicious as the 100-metre could be, we did make a few friends in our ranks. A couple of young sprinters I'd been training with in Austin were becoming truly elite. Obadele Thompson of Barbados was looking good for a medal in Sydney (he ended up taking bronze). Kareen Streete-Thompson of the Cayman Islands (born in Ithaca, New York, he'd also at times represented the U.S.) was an excellent sprinter but an even better long-jumper, winning silver at the Pan Am Games in Winnipeg. Obadele, to my mind, should have been the heir apparent to my reign as Olympic champion. He was that good. I had suggested both athletes train with Dan in Austin, and they did. That connection ended up solving a problem for Dan and me in Sydney, though I still ripped Canadian officials for causing the problem in the first place.

Dan could not get accreditation from the Canadian team as a coach so he could join his athletes on the track and help us prepare. I couldn't believe Canadian officials were shutting him out. Dan had coached the vast majority of Canadians winning medals in international track competition. He'd even trained my friend Kate, Mark's wife, a world downhill champion. Representing Canada. World. Champion. And he coached Glenroy. And he coached me. Did I need to remind the Canadian officials what I'd won for Canada while training with Dan? I guess I did, because it ended up being either Cayman Islands or Barbados that got him accreditation to be on the track.

When I saw a pair of Canadian coaches sitting at the front of the stands watching us practice, I walked over.

"Get the fuck out of here," I told them. "This is a closed practice."

They protested. I didn't care. They weren't my coaches, and as far as I was concerned they'd conspired to keep my coach out of the facility. I couldn't concentrate while they were watching. I could barely contain my anger, let alone practice.

They left. For all the things that got in my way during my athletic career, nothing gave me such consistent grief as Athletics Canada meddling needlessly in its athletes' affairs. Do you need a better example of why I went to the trouble of staging my own race at SkyDome?

A different and entirely new kind of grief was waiting for me in the morning. When I woke up, I could barely breathe. Sucking air into my lungs was hard and pushing it out was an issue. I tried to ignore the strain and drag myself through practice, but I was barely functioning. Sydney was hot, and the humid weather didn't help. Stubbornly, I didn't want to concede to whatever was happening. I hadn't come this far to be derailed.

Reality punched me in the gut during my next competition. I came off the blocks and immediately pulled up. I was gasping. It felt like somebody was suffocating me with a pillow. I stopped around the thirty-metre mark. Stubborn pride had just taken a back seat to the need to breathe.

I stumbled off the track and immediately went to the medical tent. It turned out I had bronchial pneumonia and my lungs were filled with fluid. It's hard to put my finger on what exactly caused this. To this day, I don't know. Maybe it was all too much too fast. Perhaps I was pushing my body too hard when, in fact, it needed proper rest.

As I sat on the table in the medical tent, with Mark Lindsay by my side, there was an empty feeling that pervaded my entire being. That's really the best way to describe it. All kinds of angry thoughts crossed my mind.

I was the defending Olympic 100-metre champion, and this is how I am going out?

I came all the way back from a ruptured Achilles, and this is how I am going out?

I was nearing the end of my career, and this is how I am going out?

The pneumonia that took me down in Sydney was one of the toughest pills I've ever had to swallow. I was humbled. When athletes grow older and their bodies begin to betray them, it messes with their heads. I mean, my body is the source of my greatest achievements. It has provided me with so much in this world, and I've also offered plenty to it. I've conscientiously fed my body, nurtured and trained it. I've optimized it to accomplish historic feats. And yet, when it reached a certain age, a certain degree of wear, it began to give out, whether it was my Achilles or my immune system.

I felt like a race car driver running out of gas on the second-last lap.

This is nothing personal, Donovan, I tried to reassure myself. *Dude, you're just aging.* It was time doing this, not anything I could have prevented. That was a definitive explanation and didn't leave any tiny margin for me to regret and obsess over. For all my disappointment, I could find a way to live with the hard reality of time.

I think if I hadn't made an honest attempt to be ready for Sydney and had just given up after my surgery, *then* I would have been eternally pissed off. I didn't quit, and to this day that offers me inner peace. I funded my rehab without any help from the Canadian Olympic Committee or Athletics Canada—we're talking more than $250,000 for everything from standard medical costs to chiropractor treatment, massage therapy, training facilities, medication, vitamins and food. And then I showed up at the gym every day and toiled through intense physical pain.

A single appearance at another Sydney venue buried the truth of my determination in a more salacious storyline. I'd removed myself from competition in Australia but had my eye on another Olympics. Toronto was preparing a bid for 2008. My good friend John Bitove Jr., owner and founder of the NBA Toronto Raptors, was spearheading the effort. He was in Sydney for the 2000 Games and was celebrating his fortieth birthday with dinner at a supper club in Darling Harbour. Of course, I joined him. I was out of competition, and we were in frequent conversations at the time about developing a bid that could compete with the likes of Beijing and Paris.

My head coach, Brent McFarlane, drove me to the dinner. I was spotted at the club by the press. Predictable media reports followed. They insinuated that I must have been healthy enough to compete if I was clearly well enough to attend a good party.

My priorities were suddenly up for debate. I'd nearly given my lungs to compete. I would have put my health in jeopardy at that stage of my career if it meant a medal. But sprinting was impossible. It wasn't hard, it wasn't too hard to bother—it was impossible. The uproar was stupid. My own coach had taken me to the dinner—don't you think he'd have protested if he thought I could compete? Common sense didn't prevent the insinuations from taking over the narrative.

All of these thoughts and reflections were in my head in Australia, the positive and negative. I needed to shake off my doubt and stop the existential crisis from cascading. I needed to reaffirm my goal and keep my head on track. I had gone into Australia very mindful that the 2001 world championships were taking place on home soil. If that was going to be my final appearance, I had every intention of going out a winner.

Following Sydney, I went back to Austin to retool, suspecting full well that the coming 2001 track season would be my last. I planned the year to include several of the small competitions that were among my favourite places to compete, winning a number of races in Germany, the Golden Spike in the Czech Republic; Turino, Italy; Strasbourg, France. In June, at the Canadian Championships in Edmonton, I won, securing my place on the world championship team for later that summer in the same city.

My lungs had recovered and Achilles was repaired, and I had no trouble seeing myself making the finals. Maybe this was going to be the last event of my life, but I treated it like business as usual, and I sure as hell wasn't entertaining thoughts about *any-thing* other than a podium finish. Winning was the priority.

I said to Mark, "I'm gonna let it all out." There would be no pacing of my heats and semi. If there was one more medal in my body, I was going to chase it down in Edmonton. As usual, Dan knew what I was feeling without being told. He hated travelling, but summers were quiet at the university in Austin, and he always tried to join me at the big events. But he was also well aware that this competition was one he wouldn't want to miss.

I ran 10.20 in my first heat and 10.11 in my second, good enough to advance. Then came the semis. When I got off the starting blocks, it felt like I was piloting a seven-speed car—I was shifting the gears like crazy and the car was not responding. Then, at the fifty-metre mark, I realized it was just not happening.

So, this is where it ends, I thought.

I think I came in sixth in that race. A 10.33. I didn't qualify for the final. And just like that, I decided my sprinting career was done.

I got a little teary-eyed walking off the track, and then I tilted my head and looked up at the crowd. I saw the Canadian fans rising to their feet, clapping. They knew I was hurting, maybe they saw the pain in my face or my body. And they knew me well enough to know I would never settle for results like that. They could tell it was over.

I began to jog around the track and wave to the crowd.

I used to do that while flush with the satisfaction of victory, comfortable with the knowledge that my training had done its job and I had done mine. This time, though, I had none of that emotion to carry me. But the crowd didn't let me feel that emptiness, not for a second. For the better part of a decade, I had worked through pain and some brutal lessons to give them joy. And now they were returning the favour. They stood, many sobbing, and cheered and waved flags from all over the world. It wasn't just Canadians who wanted to make sure I left the track that day with my head held high. The overwhelming gratitude I felt during that standing ovation brought more tears to my eyes. Their dedication touched me deeply. It showed me in the purest way possible what my career and leadership had meant to them.

As I continued to stroll around the track, I also saw people trackside crying—race officials, administrators and even media members from the Caribbean to places as far as New Zealand. These were folks I had built relationships with over the years, and seeing them become emotional tugged at my heart.

That night, my team—Dan and Mark and my agents—several friends and I gathered at an Italian restaurant for my retirement dinner. I was thankful that I could say a proper goodbye to the fans earlier and now to my team and friends, and especially that we could do it on home soil. Of course, I'd trusted my health, at times maybe even my life, to Mark and Dan over the years, so it was inevitable that they would be friends for the rest of my life. But this extraordinary chapter of our time together was over. Many athletes aren't afforded closure like that, whether because of injury or circumstance. I was lucky to gather with people who had supported me and so enriched my life and career.

I remember listening to races on that little radio we had back on the farm in Jamaica and being amazed at how one person could captivate a stadium that was filled to the brim with people, as well as all the people around the world listening or watching at home. One sprinter could provide drama and suspense that kept each member of the audience on the edge of their seat.

If you had told the little boy from Manchester, the fourth of five sons to George and Daisy, that that would be his legacy when he grew up, he would have thought that was pretty damn cool. Between beginning with Dan in 1994 and injuring my Achilles in 1998, I had the most successful resume of any athlete in the world. It was engrained in me that success was the only path worth considering, but I couldn't have dreamed my success would happen with the whole world watching. And now the dream was at its end.

But in other ways, life was just getting started.

CHAPTER 10

HEARTACHE

IT SAYS A LOT about a place when a man who has everything and most of his adult life ahead of him chooses to return.

I was retired at age thirty-two. I could have gone anywhere, someplace where life was always easy, someplace luxurious. No more winter and snow. No more navigating the love-hate relationship with the media. My father had taught me how to do business at a very young age, and I could have launched back into real-estate investment from anyplace I chose.

I chose Oakville. I had purchased an acreage in the southeast of the town, and that's where I built my retirement home. I still owned a loft in Austin, Texas, which I still love and feels like a second hometown, and had been flying back and forth to

Ontario while my new home was under construction. By the fall of 2002, the house was ready, and I moved to Oakville for good. I was planning to live in that house until the end of my days and still do. And my days are far from done.

Of course, I had frequented my hometown intermittently over the course of my career, but I'd never had the chance to stay for long. There were times when I was in Canada for probably just four weeks out of the entire year. I trained in the southern U.S. and travelled the world constantly to compete. Now, for the first time since the early 1990s, I could really return to my roots in the town I loved.

I had always been struck by Oakville's unparalleled blend of people. It reminded me of my own family's globe-spanning history, the variety of faces that came together at family gatherings and took such joy in being together. Oakville felt like a great big version of that, as few other places I'd seen in the world did. And the town had always reciprocated the love I showed it. The community had embraced me as soon as I arrived in 1980. My brother and I were high-school sports stars, and even back then, complete strangers would tell us that we made them proud. We could be buying doughnuts at Tim Hortons or enjoying a burger at McDonald's and other customers would pat us on the back or offer high-fives. Oakville has always championed me like a favourite son.

The city wasn't hesitant to show its pride in my accomplishments. When I returned from Atlanta with Olympic gold hanging from my neck in 1996, the town threw a party to celebrate. My father had been speaking with the mayor at the time and was instrumental in facilitating a grand parade to welcome me home. The mayor of Toronto also wanted to hold a massive parade for me, but Oakville had offered first and were determined to put on a hell of a celebration. That was good enough for me to stick with my hometown. I rode through the streets in an old Mustang convertible, and it seemed like the whole town came out to join the festivities. The sidewalks and boulevards were lined with people. My high-school friends and coaches were all there, along with anybody who mattered to me, really. My dad had a giant smile on his face that entire day. The parade culminated in Coronation Park, a picturesque spot by the shores of Lake Ontario, and I received the key to the town. Best of all, I had a trail, a park and a street named after me—the Donovan Bailey Trail, Donovan Bailey Park and Donovan Bailey Way. The trail was the same path I would ride my bike on with my pal Rick when we were kids. Some of my other friends lived on the other side of the trail. We used it every day, cutting through the park, and now, kids doing the same thing would know this route to each other's homes by my name. Not much in life has baffled me, but that honour does.

Moving back after my retirement presented a plug-and-play type scenario. All my closest friends were still living in and around Oakville, so there were days when I woke up and felt as if I was back in high school or college. Of course, now I had responsibilities. My number-one priority was another reason that returning to Oakville had been a no-brainer. My eight-year-old daughter, Adrienna, was living there with her mother. Even though my parents hadn't married and had lived separately within the same village, I had always benefitted from a closely knit family dynamic. George and Daisy never fought or raised their voices at one another, and even after they both married and Dad was in Canada, they communicated every day. That peace and stability helped me grow up with the kind of security that fosters confidence—the kind of confidence that I wanted Adrienna to benefit from as much as I had. It was my only goal to give her the same kind of foundation in childhood that had provided me with so many advantages in life.

I had sacrificed a great deal in my personal relationships during my career. The commitments and demands of being a world-class athlete kept me from all kinds of important events, from weddings of friends to milestone birthdays of my child. She was born in August—right in the middle of the track season, when I needed to be away for competitions. There was no way around that, and my absence left a pain that lingers.

One particular absence haunts me to this day. She attended St. Mildred's-Lightbourn, an all-girls school in Oakville, and one of its annual traditions was a father-daughter dance. I wasn't able to attend, and because of that, my first-born child had to sit in the gymnasium and watch her friends dance with their dads under the spotlight. I can't imagine the loneliness she felt in that moment. That alone would have been enough to convince me to retire in Oakville. During the first year back, I tried to make up for lost time, packing as much as I could into my schedule. Adrienna and I quickly established a wonderful relationship.

We had frequent date nights—just her and her old man. We went for walks and drives, and I had even once braved the ice when she took up figure skating. I didn't know how to skate, and from the moment I arrived at the rink, I was very nervous.

I was so worried that I would accidentally do the splits on the ice and shred every muscle in my lower body. I tiptoed onto the fresh sheet and, sure enough, fell right on my ass. My daughter exploded with laughter, which made it all worthwhile.

We really got to know each other, and she became 100 percent a daddy's girl. It really was the small things about fatherhood that I'd missed and were now providing the most joy, like just riding our bikes to nowhere in particular or chomping on french fries together. When it comes to the people I love the most, I've always valued quality time—the meals, the movies, the coffee, the conversation—over the ostentatious parties and events. Some of my fondest memories in life are of sitting on the floor with Adrienna to watch Pixar's *Monsters, Inc.* for the fortieth, forty-first, forty-second time in a row. We would laugh and eat popcorn, and I would eventually nod off to sleep, only to feel Adrienna poke me in the eye to rouse me. "Daddy, wake!" Those pokes weren't quite as enjoyable as Daisy's scalp massages, but I was just as grateful for the chance to have them.

I have only ever had one refuge in this world that gave me absolute comfort. I say it often because it's true: I am an unabashed mama's boy. And my mother's house never stopped feeling like home.

By the time I retired, my parents were both living in Jamaica, and I made sure to take a half dozen or more trips back each year, any time there was an opportunity. I never thought twice about where I would stay when I visited. I could walk through Daisy's front door and step away from the chaos of being recognized, criticized or treated like anything but my mother's son.

And my childhood bedroom was truly the one place in this world where I found complete refuge.

During visits after my retirement, though, I started to notice something unusual about my mom. She was repeating herself and becoming forgetful. My younger brother, Michael, was living close by and shared some of his own observations. She had started losing track of where she was and even of people's names. This was a woman who'd always remembered every minute detail about everything. In her day, mothers were just built like that—there were no handheld devices that stored an entire phonebook's worth of numbers. Daisy could easily recall and rattle off the exact digits of my phone number, along with those of my brothers, aunts, uncles, cousins and many others. Michael said she was even beginning to leave the kitchen with the stove on and forget she was cooking a meal.

She was *drifting*—that's the word that stuck with me. She was there physically, but mentally she came and went, drifting through life. Michael took her to get checked out around 2003, and it turned out she was suffering from early signs of Alzheimer's. In Jamaican culture, we don't place our elders in an institution to receive care. She continued to live at home but needed assistance with day-to-day activities, so we hired a personal support worker. As well, Michael's wife moved in to help take care of her.

I don't use the word *hate* at all. It contains a strong, negative energy, and the less of that you can have in your life, the better. Nevertheless, I HATE Alzheimer's. This disease took hold of a vibrant, healthy woman and depleted her mind to the point where she didn't recognize the greatest commodities in her life: her sons. As I'm sure anyone who has watched a loved one fall prey to dementia can attest, seeing our mother slip into that terrible state was incredibly difficult.

I began to call in favours. During my career, I had made many connections in the medical world. I called esteemed doctors and researchers from Israel, Switzerland, Austria and China, and asked their advice on Alzheimer's therapy and medication. Was there a surgery that could fix this? I would have flown with my mother to the ends of the Earth to get her the treatment required to make her well again. But all I kept hearing from these professionals, each leaders in their field, was that nothing could be done.

It makes me very sad to think back to my mother's decline. I was completely helpless, and that was frustrating beyond belief. I could do nothing but sit and watch as her mind deteriorated. I was also going through some personal issues at the time, which I'll get to, and this just depleted me. It was the hardest time of my life.

No matter her own state of mind, whenever my mother sensed I was losing myself in my thoughts, she would seek to calm me down. The final scalp massage my mom ever gave me came long after she was diagnosed. I was lying on her couch, staring at the television, when she sat down beside me, put my head in her lap and began rubbing it. Her instincts took over. It didn't matter that the disease had robbed her of memory, and it didn't matter that if you asked her, she probably couldn't have told you who I was. In this moment, something inside her remembered exactly who I was and what I needed.

The unbreakable bond between a mother and her child.

I was overwhelmed by all of that and began to cry. I was sad but also comforted. It was a feeling that I wanted to cling to and never let go.

To this day, I don't know if my mother doled out scalp massages to my brothers. That was the beauty of her character, though. She would tell me in secret that I was her favourite son. I know for a fact that she told my siblings the same thing. She would call me her "Big Son," even though I was the fourth of five. She also said that to Glenroy, Wilburn, O'Neil and Michael. However, there was no competition between us for her affection. She made each of her children feel the same unconditional love, and that was such a wonderful thing. She taught me how to communicate properly and taught me how to love. I still believe that my mother was the most perfect human being in the world.

My mom, Daisy Lewis, lived with Alzheimer's for nine years before she passed away in 2013.

I like to say that my father was very Jamaican. He was your prototypical Jamaican male and was a father in the only way he knew how: he was an authoritarian. He made rules and I was expected to follow them with precision. He steadfastly believed that his job was to give instruction to his children until they had outgrown the need for it. As I grew up and found success, my dad gradually eased off. He thawed out, I like to joke. The instructions slowly transformed into conversations. And then a strange thing happened: we became friends.

When I retired, my dad was living in Kingston, and whenever I flew back, he would pick me up at the airport. We developed a bit of a tradition: I would land, and my driver would take me directly to my dad's house so I could drop my luggage off and freshen up. I say "his" house, but all the houses in our family were like family homes, open for us all to come and go whenever we pleased. After I settled in, we would head straight to his favourite local fish restaurant by the ocean. There were some Red Stripes in the mix, of course, and sometimes even a bit of rum. It was a grand time. Just a father and his boy, sitting beneath a hut on the lush sand, gaffing about life and watching the sun set on the water's horizon. Man, it was heaven on Earth.

We became fixtures in each other's lives and did everything together. We went to concerts—we saw his favourite reggae artist, John Holt, at National Stadium in Kingston. I took him to see Floyd Mayweather box in Las Vegas, as well, continuing our lifelong habit of bonding over his favourite sport.

My dad always had keys to my homes and vehicles, so whenever he visited me in Canada he could come and go as he pleased. He would hold court with friends in my home and host Father's Day and Christmas each year, without fail. My dad and I spoke openly and honestly about everything. He would constantly tell me, "You should go to law school." This was *after* my retirement. He really believed in me. He even urged me to pursue a role in politics. I shrugged that off, but he wasn't letting it go so easily. One day we had a conversation that touched on politics, and he said, "You know what? *Senator* would sound good next to your name. Senator Donovan Bailey."

So far, I've passed on that suggestion.

One time my dad accompanied me to an autograph signing. When I introduced him to my fans, he asked them, "Would you like my autograph, too?" He had come a long way from the days when he had doubted the wisdom of my choice to pursue a career in track. The old authoritarian was forever stuck in some of his ways, though. He wouldn't tell me outright that he was proud of me. Instead, it was in a moment like this, said with a smile to some track fans, when he acknowledged I'd made good on my bet.

That was good enough for me.

My dad drank four litres of water a day and avoided fried foods entirely. He lived a very healthy lifestyle, eating plenty of vegetables and never indulging in more than one beer or glass of rum in social situations. All of that made what happened to him so shocking.

He called me one day and told me he had just gone for a checkup with his doctor, and his blood work was showing something strange. There was an issue with his kidney. I asked him what it could be, and he played down my concern. "It can't be anything," he said. "I rarely drink. I've never smoked. I eat very well." Nonetheless, I arranged for him to see a doctor who came highly recommended, and the doctor identified a small polyp on one of his kidneys.

My father and I had a conversation about it afterwards, and he was very matter-of-fact. "Oh, it's not a big deal," he said with a shrug. That chat took place in March, around his birthday, and he was more concerned about celebrating than worrying. I asked him to come up to Oakville when the weather got warmer, so he could go to a hospital in Toronto and get that kidney removed.

"It's just a kidney, Dad. You'll be good with one. We'll take the other out, and that's that."

I wish it had been that simple.

After his kidney surgery at Toronto General Hospital, we learned that my father had collecting duct carcinoma, a very aggressive cancer. Researchers didn't know much about it at the time, but it was known to affect Black people at a higher rate than average. We had hoped that removing the affected kidney would put him in the clear.

I went to the hospital every day while my father was recovering and made sure to keep his spirits high. I'd implore him to get up so we could walk up and down the halls. "Pops, let's get some exercise. Can't have you seated all day." After four days he was discharged, and he went to stay with Aunt Yvonne, the widow of my Uncle Keith, who you'll remember died of pancreatic cancer just before my gold medal race in 1996. She lived in Markham, Ontario, north of Toronto. If anybody knew how to help my dad during his recovery process, it was Aunt Yvonne.

A few days later, I was in a board meeting for a charity foundation I was involved with, when she phoned. She told me that Dad wasn't well. He was showing the symptoms of someone who'd had a stroke; he was mumbling his words, and one side of his face was drooping. Shaken by the news, I got in my car right away to collect him. We drove to Humber River Hospital, because I knew a few doctors there and it was in the north end of the city. They gave my dad an MRI, and he was transported urgently downtown to Toronto General. There, one of the doctors pulled me aside. My father hadn't suffered a stroke. It looked like the cancer had metastasized and spread all through him.

My father was eighty-two years old, and the harsh reality was that radiation treatment would destroy him. The only choice we had was to let him live this out, and what was important now was letting my dad choose where he wanted to do so. That conversation was probably the hardest one I've ever had.

He looked me in the eye and said, "Son, how the hell did I get cancer? I've lived a life where there was nothing foreign that went in my body. Nothing. How did this happen?"

We cried during that talk. Two grown men who never shed a tear around each other were now sobbing.

"I don't know, Dad," I responded. "The decision that we've got to make now is do you want to be in Canada, or do you want to go back to Jamaica, where you'll be in the sunshine?"

He just looked at me. Through his glassy eyes, I could see determination. Denial, maybe, but determination for sure.

"We're going to beat this," he said. "Let's beat this cancer."

I reached out to my connections around the world to find help, just as I had for my mom. I had friends in Israel who were involved in research on cannabidiol (CBD), and I knew prominent people in the medical field from Switzerland, across Canada and the U.S. I had lost my mother, and now I was in danger of losing my father. I had to help him in any way I could. At the end of the day, though, this was cancer we were dealing with. It had ravaged my dad's body. Naturopathic remedies like CBD oil seemed to give him comfort but could only do so much.

He decided to go to Jamaica to live out his days at his home in Kingston. There was a garden there full of fruit trees he had planted himself, including mango, grapefruit, jackfruit, apple and, of course, ackee. My father spent several months there, fighting to live. My stepmother had already passed away, but he wasn't isolated. He was on the phone every day with his youngest sister, Blossom, and his oldest sister, Hazel, and they lifted his spirits. He had a great support system and maintained a positive attitude. The beautiful Jamaican weather and environment also helped. He was always out in the garden, and whenever he felt like eating a fresh mango, he could just walk up to the tree and pluck it himself.

I flew down to spend as much time as possible with him. Watching my dad battle for life gave me a heaping dose of perspective. The phrase "You only live once" became much more than a cliché to me; you really had better make use of every single moment.

I was with both of my parents during their final days on this Earth, joking and laughing and talking and eating. I enjoyed being in their presence to the fullest, even as their illnesses led toward their inevitable conclusions. But the frustration of facing something beyond my control ate at me in a way that I'd seen before. Like the mythical weak spot for which it is named, my Achilles tendon—on the other leg—tore. I was in Oakville, between visits to see my dad, and blowing off some steam playing basketball with friends, when I suffered the injury. Not as complete a rupture as last time, and not as dire since I was now retired, but debilitating just the same. And strange. When I came away from the chaos of the SkyDome race and then left Dan and Austin for Loren and Atlanta, one Achilles blew. And now, facing my father's cancer, the other side followed. Both were circumstances that dragged out for months, during which I couldn't control the decline of things that mattered most to me.

I had surgery and, against doctor's orders, was soon flying back and forth between Canada and Jamaica with a hard cast on one leg.

And then my father passed, leaving a massive and immediate hole in my life. I was horrifically sad. To say that I missed him falls so far short of what I was feeling. I could no longer pick up the phone to call him and talk about life or boxing or his grand-children. I had lost my best friend.

On the day of his funeral, I hosted a grand celebration of life for him at his home in Kingston. His siblings and many friends showed up, as did his favourite DJ. Over food and drinks, people reminisced about what a happy person he was and how he'd greatly enhanced their lives. Grown men who are not inclined to show affection were wrapping their arms around each other. They were saying, "Man, George taught me this," or "George helped me with that."

Learning about the impact he had had on so many people really hit me. It sent me into an introspective state. My father had been such a beacon of positivity during his eighty-two years of life. I could only hope that by the time my celebration was held, I would have had that kind of impact on half as many people as he did.

The deaths of my parents changed me. It was a harsh reminder that time moves forward, and we all grow more vulnerable with each passing day. Another occurrence that enforced such thoughts was the passing of my hero, Muhammad Ali. He died in June of 2016, and I was fortunate to attend his funeral and memorial service in Louisville, Kentucky.

My friend Lennox Lewis, the undisputed heavyweight champion of the world, was invited to the funeral. I asked him if I could join him. Lennox and I had met when he was playing basketball for Kitchener against my big brother O'Neil. Lennox was a good basketball player, but a great boxer. In 1988, he won Olympic gold for Canada as a super-heavyweight. Like me, he'd moved to Canada at age twelve, and also like me he'd got so frustrated with the Canadian athletics bureaucracy, he considered leaving. He turned pro in his native England and became one of the greatest heavyweight champions ever. There have only been two Canadian athletes who were undisputed champions of the world. Neither received adequate support from his governing body, and both had to leave the country to get proper training, yet both of us wore the Canadian flag proudly. Nobody reminds me like Lennox does of the ways Canada fails to meet the opportunity when a truly exceptional talent appears.

I'd only met Ali once, but he was an important figure in my life. I had to be there, and Lennox was happy for us to attend together.

There was a global outpouring of love for The Champ when he passed, and walking into the enormous group of people assembled for his memorial was surreal. The collection of successful Black men and women in attendance was awe-inspiring. Will Smith was there, along with Mike Tyson, George Foreman, Larry Holmes and Bryant Gumbel, among others. Influential people from politics, sports and other industries were gathered to pay their respects.

In addition to respect, though, this was a time to celebrate and to educate younger people about Ali's impact on society.

He touched people of different ethnicities and religious backgrounds through his voice and his actions. He packed a lot into his seventy-four years, and I'm not even talking about his work in the ring. His activism was powerful in its own right.

Former U.S. president Bill Clinton perfectly encapsulated Ali during his eulogy:

> I think he decided something I hope every young person here will decide. I think he decided very young to write his own life story. I think he decided, before he could possibly have worked it all out, and before fate and time could work their will on him, he decided he would not ever be disempowered. He decided that not his race nor his place, nor the expectations of others, positive, negative or otherwise, would strip from him the power to write his own story. He decided first to use his stunning gifts, his strength and speed in the ring, his wit and way with words in managing the public, and his mind and heart, to figure out at a fairly young age who he was, what he believed, and how to live with the consequences of acting on what he believed. A lot of people make it to steps one and two, and still just can't quite manage living with the consequences of what they believe.

Clinton also described Ali as a "universal soldier for our common humanity." That line really stood out. I think there was a shared understanding among the Black men who were there that *this* was important. We silently took note that we all had to do our part to make the world a better place, just like Ali had. Of course, even if we all did our part, it still wasn't going to measure up to what this one man accomplished around the globe. However, that didn't mean we shouldn't try. Many of the successful Black men in attendance had strong platforms and could influence a great deal of people. If we didn't use that in a positive manner, then, ultimately, we didn't learn anything from Ali.

My dad had instilled in me the concept of always doing the right thing, and Ali was the ultimate example of a man taking that imperative to heart. Observing him throughout my life influenced me to never stray from the right side of history. How could I have shaken my idol's hand and looked him in the eye as he congratulated me on my gold medals had I cheated with PEDs, even if I'd got away with it? Sure, some of my words and actions were controversial and could look like detours from the right path—and I'll get to that shortly—but my internal compass always pointed me to where I needed to go.

The Champ rubbed off on me in so many ways. Most young athletes today are coached on how to interact with the press and are taught what to say and what not to say. It's imperative for them, because it can be very easy for a young person to step on verbal land mines that can wreak havoc on their career. Me, I never went through media training. Muhammad Ali was my coach.

During the early stages of my track and field career, I would go through my father's videotapes and study how the GOAT conducted himself during interviews. I would write down my impressions of his mannerisms and how he answered questions. Ali would listen to the reporters, take a deep breath and then deliver his message in the form of a strong, confident sound bite.

Listening to him on the radio while I was growing up in Manchester, then watching him on television in Oakville, made me want to emulate him, and I'll forever cherish the impact he had on me as a boy—the man who called *me* "Champ" in Atlanta. I don't think my athletic career would have been the same without his influence. It was a blessing to be present in Kentucky for the celebration of his incredible life.

Afterwards, I was back in Oakville, my sprinting career behind me, The Champ gone, my parents in my heart but no longer in my life. I began to find purpose in retirement that would allow me to live up to their examples. Whatever I did—business, charitable endeavours, media work—I wouldn't do it as well without the standards they'd set.

CHAPTER 11

BAILEY, INC.

MY PARENTS TAUGHT US that if you're blessed, you should give back. Muhammad Ali illustrated that to me. Countless other successful people I've encountered throughout my life did the same. There's a line in the Bible that I have always kept in mind that speaks to this point: "Remember this: Whoever sows sparingly will also reap sparingly, and whoever sows generously will also reap generously" (2 Corinthians 9:6–8).

This concept appears in some form or another among religious and spiritual teachings across the world. Even in a secular society, it holds weight. Just look at the philanthropy of Bill Gates and its impact on global health, or Warren Buffett, who pledged to donate more than 99 percent of his extraordinary wealth by the end of his life.

I have been blessed ever since I was a child, and so it was natural for me to want to share my good fortune with others who didn't enjoy the same head start in life. Even as kids, my three older brothers were paying things forward as volunteers in our church, and I followed suit. By the time I was just ten years old, I was already a junior Sunday school teacher. My father certainly had his own unique methods of giving back, and one superb example of that is the Canadian Caribbean Association he started in Oakville when he arrived in Canada. I saw first-hand how that initiative helped newcomers acclimatize to their new life. It acted as a conduit that connected immigrants to a vast local network of people in the Caribbean diaspora. My dad and stepmother helped plan fundraising events in the Greater Toronto Area through the CCA. As you might know, everyone in the Caribbean adores music and loves to dance. It doesn't matter what country you're from, Jamaica, Trinidad, Guyana or Grenada. It's like rhythm is in our blood. The dances held in Canada back in the 1970s and '80s helped provide immigrants with a slice of life from back home. They would arrive at the hall wearing thick winter coats, step through the doors and hear reggae music blasting from the speakers. It made the harsh, unforgiving Canadian winter palatable to them for a moment, because it was like they were being transported back to the islands. I know for a fact that some men and women met their spouses at the events put on by my father. Imagine generations of Canadian families tracing their genesis back to unions forged at the parties you organized. To me, that is the ultimate form of giving back.

After I retired, I also became more focused on philanthropy. The fame afforded me by those gold medals meant I had many opportunities to help people, and I threw myself into several causes over the next two decades, including those related to Alzheimer's and cancer. I've supported the Alzheimer Society of Canada, was an ambassador for a charity in the U.K. called Go Dad Run, which was started by my good friend from Wales, Colin Jackson, world-champion hurdler and still world-championship record holder, and raised awareness and funds for Prostate Cancer UK. Cancer and Alzheimer's stole my parents from this world, and I know the pain they wreak on families. So, if there was anything I could contribute to research and to helping others who were afflicted, you could bet I was going to be involved. I get a lot of requests for appearances and charity initiatives, and any ask involving Alzheimer's or cancer automatically moves to the top of my list.

Mentorship is closely tied to philanthropy and the desire to give back to the community. They go hand in hand. My father was the most important mentor in my life. Dan was number two, as I became the greatest sprinter on Earth under his guidance. He was such a beautiful teacher, though, that his guidance didn't stop with athletics. Our conversations would veer into his vast knowledge about the stock market, economy, politics and even fatherhood. When he became a grandfather, Dan shared with me what a pleasure it was to spoil his grandchildren without having to parent them, after putting in so much hands-on effort with his own kids. To this day, our conversations have no limits and extend to every subject. We stay in touch often, and I still soak up everything he has to say.

Dan passed the baton to me, in a sense, and that is the phrase I chose for one of my charity initiatives, which falls under the umbrella of the Donovan Bailey Foundation. The premise is that if you're a successful Canadian, you can share your knowledge and experience with someone younger. It doesn't matter what your profession is—lawyer, mechanic, car salesperson—you can pass things down to others who might not otherwise have a chance to learn them. The wisdom you've gathered and the education and experience you've amassed shouldn't benefit just you; it should benefit the world. I feel strongly about that.

I really enjoy working with kids. I've always had a strong connection to children and take pride in being authentic with them. Kids can see through any BS that comes their way from elders, and I've found that they embrace me when I speak my truth, because transparency comes naturally to them. They have no filter in how they express their feelings and appreciate when the authenticity is reciprocated. Some adults might feel that I'm being arrogant and abrasive when, in fact, I'm just being open. If I'm going to talk to kids about track and field, I'm not going to affect some false humility with them. They're talking to one of the fastest people who has ever ran across the surface of the planet, and any attempt to speak like I'm something other than that is going to feel fake to them. That's no way to talk to kids.

I confess to experiencing a selfish joy in mentoring kids, motivating them and imploring them to aspire toward big goals.

I derive great meaning from the idea that I can help someone change their life. There have been many times when fans have walked up to me, tapped me on the shoulder and said, "Mr. Bailey, I met you when I was a kid." Maybe I signed an autograph or took the time to speak with them when they were children, and now, after many years, sometimes decades, they can recount to me how much of a positive impact that encounter had on them.

One such encounter really stands out. I was dining at a restaurant in Oakville one day long after my retirement, when a man came up to me. He was a dentist in Florida and was visiting his family in Ontario during the Christmas holidays. I didn't recognize him, but he said we had met years ago when he was a teenager and I was playing a pickup basketball game at Sheridan. He recalled how I had given him advice about chasing his dreams. It turned out that not long after that, he went to school in northern Illinois on a track scholarship. He took an interest in dentistry while in the States and changed course, which led to his successful career in that profession.

"I didn't know I was at a crossroads when I met you," he said. "But you talked to me about life and goals, and that changed my path. Thank you," he said.

I've seen that gentleman a few times now, and he never fails to thank me for my help. I didn't do much, but I think the impact I had on him speaks to my outlook in life. Whenever I was stopped by someone, I always felt it was important to take the time to have a proper conversation with them, listen to what they had to say and answer as authentically as possible. Because you never know when it's going to come back.

On some occasions, it wasn't even a physical meeting that impacted a young person, but rather something they saw me say on television that changed their life in some way. Some people have told me that I was somehow involved in their journey to become a doctor, lawyer or physiotherapist: "You don't understand what your winning meant to me. You don't understand what your interviews meant. You don't understand what you beating Michael Johnson meant to my personal self-esteem." I mean, come on. Hearing things like that always caused me to go home with a smile on my face.

I understood what they were saying, though, because of how Ali had inspired me as a kid. When I was older, I watched Michael Jordan, and he was a source of motivation. I even observed Tiger Woods—who is younger than I am—in the 1990s and drew certain things from his story and life, like his ability to build and manage his brand. Tiger Woods became an ambassador for golf. While Jordan played in a team sport, Tiger was a solo competitor. That really spoke to me, as a competitor in and ambassador of track and field.

I've come to understand the power of that type of influence, and it's coloured my interactions, both private and public. I'm always thinking about the little kid who might be watching me, whether I'm at the gas station or in front of cameras. I've developed a strong principle from that thought, one that boils down to a simple question I always try to ask myself: Am I delivering something that the younger version of me would have loved to hear? If the answer is no, then what I'm doing or saying requires re-evaluation.

It wasn't always that way for me. If I'm going to talk about mentorship, then I have to mention my mistakes. It's important to acknowledge transgressions and admit when you're wrong, or people won't have any faith in the other things you say. There were times when I was certainly wrong.

In 1998 I was involved in a car accident in which I crashed into a concrete utility pole. The vehicle flipped over and caught fire. I did not report the accident and was subsequently fined $200 for that. Speeding was the cause of that incident, and in 2001, I was fined $975 for driving 200 kilometres per hour, double the speed limit, on the QEW, the highway between Toronto and Oakville. I had a habit of speeding. I was still fairly young and felt invincible, still riding the high of my Olympic championships, but there is absolutely no excuse for such reckless behaviour and the grave danger it puts others in. I am sincerely sorry for it.

Dan used to tell me I needed to "clean out my closet" before training, and I feel I need to do the same upon entering this stage of my life. It is imperative, and maybe even overdue, that I clear the air. The high-speed accident in 1998 and the fine were not my only driving-related mistakes. I pled guilty in 2014 to driving with a blood alcohol level over the legal limit.

Two years prior, I had attended a charity wine-tasting event in Richmond Hill, which is just north of Toronto. Shortly after midnight, I was headed back to the city on the Don Valley Parkway and needed to take a business call—I was negotiating a contract that was tied to my work during the 2012 Summer Olympics in London. I needed to focus, so I pulled over to the side of the highway to speak on my mobile. A police officer approached my car and spoke to me. I was eventually charged and fined $1,500.

I was embarrassed by that and still am. I regret driving home after an event that was all about alcohol. I'll own that. If there is one silver lining, though, it's that those situations, like other losses and failures in my life, are a chance to learn. I paid the price legally, emotionally and psychologically. I lost some sponsors, and the entire situation affected my branding and businesses. But I did come out on the other end with a different mentality. I learned—the hard way—that I had fallen into a pattern of taking my stature for granted. If I truly wanted to be a role model to others, then I needed to immediately take a more responsible attitude toward my own conduct. And so, going forward, I became more conscious of doing the right thing.

I do think that I'm constantly evolving as a person. That's a key ingredient in life: being able to adapt as you grow. I've tried to rise to the demands of my role as a person of influence, as well as my roles as a businessman and father. I will never say I'm perfect, but I am proud that I've been able to learn from my mistakes and set an example for my three boys, Marcus, Maximus and Mateus, and my daughter, Adrienna, that life has no limits.

If you Google me, you will also find 2018 reports about my tax contributions. This is a story that needs to be set straight, not a failure of judgment on my part that I need to acknowledge. Let me explain. I had an athletic trust that contained my sponsorships and prize money that I'd earned over the years when I was sprinting. When it came time to collapse that trust, there were tax implications, so I enlisted help from one of Canada's top banks and was referred to a Toronto tax lawyer named Stuart Bollefer from the renowned firm Aird & Berlis. Bollefer courted my investment very actively. He took me to dinner several times. He invited me to golf at his country club. Tax law was certainly not my area of expertise. I asked him repeatedly to confirm that his proposals for managing my money were sound. After he had courted my business for three years, I was convinced. I hired Bollefer and followed his advice. He became my tax expert, and I listened to him the way I listened to Dan before a race. I moved offshore for a while, had no Canadian driver's licence, all according to his plan. According to the Canada Revenue Agency, though, the tax vehicle that Bollefer recommended I use was not legitimate after all. I was ordered to pay a massive amount of additional taxes to the government. I subsequently sued Bollefer and Aird & Berlis, and they settled, paying off the debt and paying me for damages, as well.

I had received and followed flawed advice. It was not unlike the more recent situation involving Usain Bolt, who lost millions of dollars to what was reported as large-scale fraud. He also received flawed advice from a private wealth management company. I wasn't even the only championship-level Canadian athlete embroiled in this. As I mentioned earlier, Kate Pace Lindsay, wife of Dr. Mark Lindsay, was an alpine skier who was once world champion and named Canada's female athlete of the year. She also hired Bollefer and then faced the same tax issues with the government as I did. There were several other high-net-worth Canadians similarly effected by this, but as highly public figures our troubles made headlines.

While we were both found innocent of any wrongdoing, I think it's important to point out how our situations were reported in different ways by the media. I write about this now because it still upsets me deeply. I remember seeing a headline about Kate that read, "Skiing Legend Cruises to Court Victory over Lawyer." Meanwhile, the coverage about me carried a vastly different tone. The *Toronto Star* wrote on June 11, 2018, that I, facing that tax bill, would "soon be left destitute." Look up the meaning of the word *destitute*. That was highly exaggerated, and totally untrue. I was being portrayed as just another Black athlete who had never learned what to do with money when he was making it and was living hand to mouth now that his big paydays were done.

I'd never fit that stereotype, but there it was. It was crystal clear that I was being painted as living on the brink of poverty because I am Black, where Kate received more sympathetic treatment because she's white. This isn't about Kate, of course. She's one of my dearest friends, and she knows better than anyone what misery that whole episode was for anyone involved. But it triggered something more for me, because it reminded me of my conversations with my father many years ago about the passive-aggressive racism that existed in Canada. That had been in the 1990s, and unsurprisingly, I guess, those prejudices were still lingering in my country nearly three decades later. Coded language was still rife, only it was updated to fit a new standard. Was *destitute* just the 2010s version of slapping *Jamaican-Canadian* in front of my name?

Racism with a smile.

People ask me all the time how my time as a champion athlete of global renown helped me in the boardroom, and my answer surprises them: it was the other way around. My time in business helped me succeed on the track.

Remember, I had spent time working in the financial district in Toronto before even committing to sprinting, and that experience helped me understand the meaning of a brand. As my star rose in track and field, I quickly became a brand myself. I already had, at the outset of my sprinting career, some base knowledge of what branding entails: managing the personality that others see in a way that allows me to put that image to good use, be it in business partnerships or philanthropy. That's branding, and a large component of it is simply making yourself available. I couldn't be a recluse or pop up every now and then, whenever I felt like it. If part of your business value is in your brand, then you've got to have a strong, enduring presence in whatever it is that you're undertaking. If it's sprinting, then you've got to talk to the media that covers track. You can't dodge reporters' questions. If it's investing in a startup, then you've got to be at the launch event, smiling and posing for pictures and signing autographs, using your public profile to draw positive attention to the initiative. I never say no to those activities. It's part of my value proposition when I sign on to a new enterprise, and I don't hesitate to make my brand part of my contribution to the enterprise's success. And if I don't want my brand associated with something, I don't get into business with it. From sports-oriented sponsors Adidas and Powerade to big-business partners such as Air Canada, McCain and Maple Leaf Foods, I endeavoured to attach my brand exclusively to blue-chip companies.

The track and field world can be tricky to navigate if you don't know how to play the game within. Most sprinters are looked at as just another athlete. There's a business model that takes these men and women for granted. It uses them to promote competitions while they are hot, and when they inevitably age and become slower, they're traded in for newer, younger models. There are always going to be thousands of hungry athletes grinding for a shot at Olympic glory; discarding older athletes is done at zero cost to athletic organizations.

However, if as an athlete you can brand yourself well, then you can carve out a slice of the pie to keep for yourself long after retirement. You can avoid just fading into memory and, instead, become a figure with a lasting presence. That's how I view myself. I became a global ambassador for sport. The day I made the decision to fully commit to track and field was the day that I started "Bailey Inc.," and I ran my life in sport as a business.

You can look through the sporting landscape and spot many athletes who are in similar positions. Michael Jordan might be the most prevalent example, but LeBron James, Tiger Woods and Floyd Mayweather have also carved out their own slices. Include the music world in this conversation and there are even more examples. Michael Jackson and Prince did it in the 1980s and '90s, while Jay-Z is among the more recent artists to become a full-blown business. And he bucked the odds to do that, becoming the first hip-hop star to ascend well beyond his genre. He captured the idea perfectly in his remix of Kanye West's 2005 "Diamonds from Sierra Leone" with this line: "I'm not a businessman. I'm a *business*, man. Let me handle my business, damn."

Once I retired from competitive sprinting, the transition back to the business world was seamless for me. I knew the terrain, and I knew what it was always looking for. I invested in various startups, such as a footwear company called Biopods, a hot sauce manufacturer called The Great Canadian Sauce Company, and software companies Arise and Javelin. I continued developing my restaurant chain, Philthy McNasty's, which I'd started in 1994 with four partners, and which we expanded to twenty locations before I sold my share. I dived headfirst into charity initiatives and real estate, an area I had plenty of experience with given my handling of my father's portfolio many years ago. I also took some calculated risks—and once again, in that story was a chance to learn from my mistakes.

I opened a high-performance clinic in Oakville and poured a great deal of money into the operation. The idea was to hire a collection of the very best wellness practitioners in the country—doctors, naturopaths, physiotherapists, chiropractors, etc.—and house them under one roof to offer privatized care. It was called Core Health and Rehabilitation, and I had ambitious plans to develop the proof of concept and expand with franchises across Ontario and ultimately go public and place locations across Canada. Once I had it running smoothly, I'd eventually sell the entire business.

I was working with a business partner on the project, and we split the duties. I was responsible for financing the project—I spent $1.7 million of my own money—and securing physical rehabilitation equipment, which I acquired by approaching my vast network of athletic-equipment suppliers. His responsibilities lay more in the hiring and day-to-day operations. This man,

Scott Anderson, was a friend of many years. We had met during his time working on the medical team with the national track squad. He wasn't just an acquaintance; I had stayed at his house and we had done family things together. I trusted him. And that blew up in my face. His business acumen was not where it needed to be for an idea so far ahead of its time, and he tanked the business.

True story: I wanted to confront him and drove to the house he was renting in Burlington, Ontario. When I pulled up to the driveway, I was met with a "For Lease" sign in the window. It turned out that he had packed up his family and skipped town. So, I ended up taking him to court and won.

The experience wasn't for naught, though. I applied my afore-mentioned mantra—*there is no such thing as failure*—and gleaned an incredible lesson. I was making an emotional investment with money in the project, and that type of endeavour is impossible to see through to the finish line. As well, I had got away from the attention to detail that I had employed to great success in the sprinting world, where I kept a tight circle and didn't let many others in. With this high-performance clinic, though, I had loosened my grip and didn't vet my team as closely as I should have. I didn't put the right people in place to achieve the results I wanted.

As thrilling as the business world might be, it could never replace the rush of competitive sprinting. Adrenalin is a hell of a drug, and I only truly felt it during competition. I loved the pressure and the challenge of breaking someone down men-tally over the course of qualifying heats, before finally beating them in a head-to-head final. I think all world-class athletes are forced to confront this void in their life once they hang up the jersey or spikes. It's human nature to miss environments in which you thrived. Golf can only give you so much of a high. Retirement falls well short of the intense situations you were once optimized to dominate, and it leaves you craving more. That's why you hear so many stories of retired athletes getting into trouble. They're desperate for something that can push them beyond their limitations, the way they once pushed themselves every day in training and competition. The real thing doesn't last forever, and it doesn't come back when you're driving the kids to school or grocery shopping on a Tuesday night. Maybe that's what I was looking for when I used to drive so fast, but it was a poor substitute.

Post-retirement I also started a sports-management company called DBX. I didn't have time to run it on a daily basis, which was essential to my concern for my reputation, so I sold the book of business, although I still own the company. More recently, I joined a consortium led by Los Angeles producer Neko Sparks to buy the Ottawa Senators of the NHL. It included several other notable investors, most famously rapper Snoop Dogg and Canadian comedian Russell Peters, to raise a billion-dollar bid for the team against three other high-profile bids. It's exciting and competitive, and it gets the juices flowing to be involved in a business endeavour of this magnitude.

Broadcasting has added some more adrenalin to my life. I took it on shortly after I retired and began to take on more work as a television analyst as I grew older. If we're talking about the evolution of a person, broadcasting was a natural progression for me. It just made sense. I got to sit in front of the cameras and translate the inner workings of sprinting to an audience in a simple, straightforward manner. I had climbed every rung of that world, and so my insight came naturally and had great value in sports media. And I still get to know the new young sprinters and stay in touch with them. I know and can translate what the competitors are doing on the track and the ways they're competing with each other that fans can't always see, even if the sprinters are nicer to each other now than we were in my day. Glenroy is managing, and I love seeing my old friend guide a group of young sprinters to new heights. Delivering on live television didn't make me nervous. I felt at home on camera. I might as well have been talking about sports on my living-room couch.

Since retirement, I formed a great relationship with the CBC and became a trusted analyst. They hired a performance coach named Bob Babinski to work with me, and he still helps me as a friend and coach to this day. I'd noticed that when I took the podium for a corporate speech, I was fully comfortable. My comfort on camera was a bit like my early comfort on the track. I could go a long way without much training, but it took a savant like Dan to coach me into a champion. Bob became my broadcast savant. He was responsible for training hundreds of media presenters and corporate executives. He analyzed my camera work and helped me get rid of the excess "ums" and "ahs" in my speech. We would work through exercises designed to polish my cadence and delivery. We were very much in sync, and I took my craft seriously, treating it the same way I treated my weight-training and nutritional regimen when I was working with Dan at LSU. I became semi-obsessed, and the continual improvement stoked my inner flame. I began to organize and measure my words even when I wasn't on the air. I could be having drinks with my friends at a bar, and I would be taking mental notes and critiquing my speech and delivery during our conversation.

Podcasting is a fresh, innovative area in media, and I've surfed that wave with my show, *Donovan Bailey Running Things: The Podcast.* It's a chance to relax and talk track and whatever else comes up while having a little more fun than traditional broadcasting allows, like we're at the bar with friends.

My experience with some members of the media was contentious during my athletic career, but now that I'm on the other side, as a media figure in my own right, I have a better understanding of how I was covered and how journalists operate. Essentially, they participate in their own Olympics, which is every major event that they cover. They're constantly competing with reporters from other outlets, and oftentimes, the best headline or story wins the proverbial gold. There's a great deal of competition in the field, and in addition to breaking stories, journalists must find different ways to cultivate an audience and keep them interested. Viewers, listeners and readers are ultimately the boss I need to keep entertained and informed.

Of course, some things are harder to change. Once, after filming at the CBC building in downtown Toronto, I joined some of the other sports broadcasters for a drink at the nearby Ritz-Carlton hotel. There, I fell into conversation with a former hockey executive who had also turned to broadcasting. He was talking about star defenceman P.K. Subban, a rare Black NHL player whose father came from Jamaica. P.K. was an All-Star and award winner at his position. He also dressed like he had read a fashion magazine sometime in the past twenty years, unlike most hockey players during that time. This former executive wondered to me why does P.K. need to wear a pink suit? Can't he just be like everyone else and wear normal clothes? Why does he always need to be noticed? I tore into the executive. Why are you even talking about what he wears? Or what he looks like or what he eats, for that matter? He's a Norris Trophy winner! He's a great looking guy. He shows up for work every day and excels, so what do you care about what he wears? A Black athlete can't stand out? Maybe everyone else should take the hint and dress better. The women at the table nodded in agreement; they knew what it was to be scrutinized for things that had nothing to do with their job performance. P.K.'s retired now and works as a broadcaster. Looks like standing out served him well.

My favourite moment in the booth came when I was working as an analyst for the CBC during the 2008 Olympics in Beijing. Of course, that was the year of Usain Bolt, the greatest sprinter who's ever lived.

The Bird's Nest stadium was supercharged with energy on the day that he sprinted the 100-metre. I was very comfortable in that setting, since I had been in a similar position in Atlanta as Usain was that day. Everybody knew that Usain—a tall, lanky, Jamaican phenom, who was twenty-one years old at the time— was going to do something special. He was already the world-record holder, having sprinted the 100-metre in 9.72 seconds during a competition in New York earlier that year.

My Olympic record of 9.84 still stood. But with Usain having already beaten my marks and now appearing in Beijing in top form, it seemed inevitable that he was going to crush my Olympic record. He did so in typical Usain Bolt fashion, sprinting an astounding 9.69 to capture his first Olympic gold medal.

The new Olympic record holder was walking past our broadcast booth after the race, when I put my hands up to my head as if to take off an imaginary crown and place it on him. He just flashed that trademark smile of his. I was so happy for him. He was a good, hard-working kid with an effervescent personality. He was an excellent role model, and if anyone was going to break my Olympic record, I was glad it was him. He was authentic in everything he did and was great with people, fans and media alike. Usain has proved to be a great ambassador of our sport.

He loved it, too, living and breathing sprinting. I might be biased, because we're both Jamaican, but none of Usain's demeanour in front of the camera was false. I always enjoyed watching him, in part because he reminded me of myself. He exuded such calm and never appeared to be anything other than chilled out and relaxed. Yes, Usain was a physical anomaly, but he also made optimal use of his talents. Anybody can be physically gifted. Really, that's not up to us. But what is under our control is how we perform when the lights are shining at their brightest. Usain showed up and was able to brush any type of pressure off his shoulders like it was dust. That's precisely what separates Olympic champions from the rest.

During our playful pseudo-coronation moment, several sports luminaries—including Linford Christie, John McEnroe, Lennox Lewis and Carl Lewis—were in the crowd, next to the CBC booth, and when Usain walked up, it was like he had joined the club. If a photo exists of that, I want it.

———

I'm glad for Usain Bolt, that he emerged as a star into a world that was ready to embrace his large personality and unprecedented talent. There was a brief period in 2002 when it looked like the Canadian athletics world was finally ready to embrace my legacy in the same spirit.

In August that year, I visited the COC office in Toronto, recently renamed from the previous title, Canadian Olympic Association, by its new CEO, a television producer and entrepreneur (co-founder of TSN) named Jim Thompson. I didn't know it, but Thompson was starting to gain a reputation for supporting the country's most successful athletes.

I had just returned from England, where I'd taken part in the opening ceremonies of the Commonwealth Games in Manchester. It was a very cool experience, of exactly the sort that Canada had not been nominating me to participate in previously. During the ceremony, I received the ceremonial torch from another recently retired champion, Stephen Redgrave, who'd won gold as a rower for England in five consecutive Olympics. I then passed the torch to star footballer David Beckham, who passed it to Queen Elizabeth II, whom I also got to meet while there. It was my agent who did the deal to get me to London, but as it turned out it seems fitting that I had a chance to represent Canada in an event like that during Thompson's brief tenure at the COC.

Given my rocky relationship with the organization, I'd scheduled a quick half hour for our meeting in Toronto. I had no idea where the office was. I had never had a reason to care. I really didn't expect much good to come of the meeting. To my amazement, Thompson and I spent five hours together. He had extensive plans to incorporate me into committee initiatives, as I was at the time probably the country's most recognizable ambassador for sport. Our meeting was epic. Sadly, within a week of our meeting, he died of a heart attack.

Beyond that very positive day we spent together, I didn't know Thompson. But I went to his funeral anyway. I spoke to his wife and let her know that her husband had been the only executive of the COC ever to call me. I had been enormously impressed by the man. And though I didn't know it then, his call was the last I'd get from the COC for nearly two decades more.

That second call finally came in April 2019 from David Shoemaker. It was telling that my meeting over coffee with the recently appointed CEO was arranged by our mutual friend, the very successful investor Sunir Chandaria. So distant was my relationship to Canadian athletics that it took a connection from my business life to bring us together. No matter how it happened, I was quickly glad it did. Shoemaker committed to forging a better relationship between the committee and me, but not just me. He wanted to create a better path for future elite athletes so my experience would never be repeated by current and future generations of Canadian champions.

That's how you start to make amends, and I'm all in on helping him make it happen. But of course, there's a lot of ground to be made up, of which I would soon be reminded.

I never thought I'd turn down a medal.

The Order of Canada is the highest civilian honour one can achieve in my country. There are three levels to it, with Companion being the highest, followed by Officer and Member.

In late 2021, Bruny became a Member for his contributions to our nation.

The Order of Canada officials wanted to appoint me as well, but I resisted, because I felt that the other members of our 1996 Olympic gold-medal-winning relay team—Glenroy, Robert and Carlton—should go in too. Bruny's highest accomplishment came from the Atlanta relay, where he earned his only Olympic gold. So, what about the other guys? They'd achieved that same height in our sport, wearing our nation's colours. I had a problem with that and decided to take a stand. I had nothing against Bruny—he deserves the honour for what he did during his sprinting career and his philanthropy.

"Go ahead without me," I told the officials.

To complicate matters, they wanted to give me the Member honour too, which I also didn't like. For over a decade, I reigned as the number-one sprinter in the history of the world, and they wanted to give me what amounted to a bronze medal? No, sir. That didn't fall in line with the champion's mindset I'd cultivated throughout my entire track and field career. And it sure as hell didn't fit my brand.

Maybe I'm still the little why kid from Manchester, never content to just accept that things are the way they are. I want an explanation. Why does Canada preserve its bureaucrats and suppress its best athletes? Why does the guy who dragged Canada out of its post-Seoul shame and back to the top of the podium—who said "own the podium" decades before it was our Olympic slogan—not have a statue somewhere? Frankie Fredericks does, in Namibia. Small country, proud of its best and not afraid to show it. Why did Ben Johnson get the Order of Canada after becoming world champion, but I didn't get it until decades after doing that, plus the Olympic gold and world record, plus actually getting to keep them all? I asked why Bruny was made *chef de mission* for Paris 2024 and was told Athletics Canada needed an Olympic leader who could speak the host country's language. Really? Did Curt Harnett speak Portuguese in Rio in 2016? Did Catriona Le May Doan speak Mandarin in Beijing in 2020? When the CEO of Athletics Canada reached out to me after I retired, saying she wanted to find a role for me, I wondered why no one was asking me to do her job. I'd run businesses. How many athletes given these high-profile leadership positions and ambassadorships have done that? Nothing against them, but they aren't me. People will celebrate me, but will they elevate me? Why haven't I been asked?

Because I've been called difficult? Because people don't want to deal with someone from outside the system asking difficult questions? Don't be like Donovan, people have said my whole career. Don't be like him how, don't win? When Dave Chappelle got Covid, his haters piled on. He came back with a quote that I've held close: "When a hero stumbles, the cowards rejoice. Nothing feels better to a coward than to watch a brave guy fall." I've been brave, and I've stumbled, once or twice. And the cowards have tried to write me off. After my Achilles tear in 1998, I heard lots of grumbling that people hoped they wouldn't need to put up with me any more. And I'm sure lots of people saw those first headlines about the tax troubles and took pleasure in thinking I'd finally got what I deserved. No chance.

I'm monumentally proud of what I've done, and of the people I've been able to count to help me do it, proud that people like

Dan and Mark have been able to grow their own exceptional careers based on our success together. Proud of my parents for the tough decisions they made so I could thrive in Canada. Proud of my kids. Maybe pride isn't the reason I said no to the Order of Canada, but it was pride that brought me around to changing my mind. I just wish the proudest people of all could have been in the room when I got it.

I spoke to some friends in federal politics, and they advised me to soften my stance on the Order. They said these politics weren't worth it in the end, so I should just accept. They had a point. I'd spent my entire athletic career pushing through the constant headwinds of the Canadian sports governing bodies, and while I emerged above it all, why should I continue that fight into my retirement? Also, even though I'd received the Order of Ontario in 2016, I was convinced that my father would have been absolutely thrilled for me to have the Order of Canada affixed to my name.

So, we split our positions down the middle, and it was announced in the summer of 2022 that I would be invested as an Officer of the Order.

I was bothered by more than just the sense that I was receiving a silver medal despite having been the greatest sprinter in the history of the world; it was also that my father was not alive to see it happen. I know he would have done anything to be there in Ottawa, front and centre with my mom, to watch as I was presented with my insignia. He would have been in his element with a permanent smile affixed to his face and my Olympic gold medals around his neck. I know he would have been snapping plenty of photos with his phone so that he could later show them off to his friends.

Everywhere I went in Canada, people assumed that I'd already been awarded the Order of Canada in 1995, after becoming world champion, like Ben Johnson had. I always thought I didn't need the Order of Canada. I just needed those two simple words I heard from fans wherever I met them: "thank you."

My life has been full of accolades, but I know the Order would have stood out to him. My father was a man who embodied fatherhood and responsibility, and he went about his business in meticulous fashion. He used every tool he was born with and acquired through his life experience to make sure that his sons were productive members of society. This honour represents him and the sacrifices he made in moving from Jamaica to Canada to support his family, and then laying a foundation for me to build on after he brought me north. You can draw a direct line between his hard work and his son becoming one of the greatest athletes in the world.

My parents might not have been present when I received the phone call about my Order of Canada appointment, however they *were* with me. I've told this to many people: my parents are my guardian angels, and they'll always be by my side. I know they were smiling, somewhere, when the call came.

Many have asked me over the years if I thought it should have come earlier. My answer has always been a resounding yes! But that's beside the point. I didn't look at the Order of Canada as any type of validation. I have already been validated by Canadian sports fans. When they tell me that they were on the edge of their seats while watching me compete, or that I was their favourite athlete, I feel it in my heart. They were the ones who always had my back and supported me through the many waves of my career.

If, as I said before, they were the boss and I was an employee of theirs, then you could call me a company man. I took pride in being a *Canadian* sprinter, and I'd like to think it showed. The greatest honour that any athlete can get is being serenaded by the national anthem of their country. I got that many times. In those moments, I was standing in front of an audience in an arena, but also an international audience watching on television. It was almost like getting married in front of the world to your country. I cherished that.

I was talking to a man in his mid-thirties recently, and he revealed that he grew up watching me. Then he said something that made me pause: "I learned from you that if you work your ass off, you can talk about winning; you can talk about being number one; you can talk about being the champion; you can talk about kicking ass.

"As well, you can also talk about being Canadian."

I thought deeply about his statement, and it made sense to me. When I was a teenager, the athletes from Canada all tended to conduct themselves in the same manner. They were going to show up and compete hard, but they were also going to be nice. They were going to speak to the media afterwards and stifle their competitive personalities. They might have had the fire burning inside them, but they didn't want to show it. They would rather apologize.

Not me. After I was misquoted in that 1996 *Sports Illustrated* article, a lot of media coverage focused on people's interpretations of my reality and not on my reality and the realities of BIPOC communities as we really lived them. No dialogue followed, no conversation with me about *why* I said what I did. 1996 was a different time, yet when it comes to systemic biases and institutional racism we still have a way to go.

The media climate after the Atlanta Olympics was driven by mainstream media; athletes could not use social media to reach out to their public directly. Unedited. Not whitewashed. Athletes today have greater control over their NIL.

Many approached me to tell my story, but many didn't want *my* story. They preferred to continue with a narrative they had constructed, or a narrative that supported their conscious or unconscious bias, a narrative that was *not* me. Part of my story *is* that conversation that should have happened after the *SI* article. In fact, it should have happened during the Dubin Inquiry, so the public could understand how a person's identity could be hyphenated and their citizenship stripped by those who wrote the headlines.

I am not a community organizer, like my father, but I always listen to learn. Conversations about racism are uncomfortable, but they don't need to be. I hope my experiences, my truths, can inspire conversations that help dismantle institutional racism and promote sport, physical activity and recreation.

I've always focused on my job, what I need to do to succeed. I made personal sacrifices in my pursuit of excellence, and I continued after the *SI* article to bet on and invest in myself. So in the interest of explaining my reality, I want to share a concept that has always helped me understand what I've been up against. A concept I've alluded to a few times in this book.

Track includes events decided in seconds, as well as throws and jumps measured in distances. In these competitions you'll always see a flag on the sidelines. Athletes like me compete outdoors, exposed to the elements, and that flag is there to detect an invisible challenge we face that can directly impact our times and speed: the wind. For a sprinter, invisible headwinds add resistance, while tailwinds push us towards the finish line.

This is any easy concept to grasp in sport. Running into the wind requires more work and can slow you down, while running with a tailwind can add to your speed. In sprinting, we acknowledge the advantage of tailwinds of as little as +2.0 metres per second, but people struggle with the idea of headwinds as they apply to real life, in particular for racialized communities.

I often wonder why that is. Colonizers created systems and institutions for their betterment, and over time history (or herstory—momma's boy and girl dad) has shown us that people who don't look like those who created and lead many of our institutions are not just overlooked, but these systems can create obstacles—headwinds—that are invisible but very real in their impact.

Acknowledging headwinds exist doesn't mean you are guilty of hateful or hurtful acts. Acknowledging experiences exist that some don't see but others feel is the first actionable step if we are to remedy indifference, promote dialogue and understanding, and bring about change. I believe that if officials and leaders acknowledged my experiences after the *SI* article, inclusion in sports in Canada would be further ahead. My closest friends are a cross-section of the world's races and cultures, and the bid I joined for the Ottawa Senators, along with other men of colour, was motivated in significant part by a desire from a leadership perspective to ensure an inclusively run organization that would set a new standard for a mostly white league, team staff, players, the community and minor league hockey clubs everywhere. The fact that I heard some people thought we had too much colour demonstrates more work is needed.

I've been doing that work for decades. And backing off or slowing down just aren't in my nature.

I've been called brash and arrogant and many other names, because of the way I approached my athletic career. But I wasn't fazed. Not even by the haters; they took the time to tell me what they thought, which I took then and take now as acknowledgment of what was beyond any doubt.

I was the very best—world champion, Olympic champion, world-record holder. World's fastest man.

Undisputed.

ACKNOWLEDGEMENTS

After reading *Undisputed*, you know how much I value the small group of people who helped me take my track career to the pinnacle of athletic achievement. It took a dedicated group to make this book happen, as well. Many thanks to all my old friends who reminded me of stories I hadn't told in many years—Glenroy, Mark and Kate, Dan, and others—and to people like my book agent, Michael Levine, and Random House Canada publisher Sue Kuruvilla, senior editor Craig Pyette and designer Matthew Flute, who shared their expertise in publishing my story. I also want to acknowledge the valuable academic contributions of Steve J. Jackson, author of "Exorcizing the Ghost: Donovan Bailey, Ben Johnson and the Politics of Canadian Identity"; Kyle T. Beatty, author of "Black Track Stars: A Reflection of Racism within the Canadian Sporting Realm"; and Tom Gilovich and Shai Davidai, authors of "The Headwinds/Tailwinds Asymmetry: An Availability Bias in Assessments of Barriers and Blessings," an article that put into words things I'd been feeling for years and offers language I have relied upon to express myself in *Undisputed*.

INDEX

DONOVAN BAILEY is a global sports legend. Named Sprinter of the Decade (1990s) by *Track and Field,* he is the first man to be 100-metre world champion, Olympic champion and world record holder at the same time. His indoor 50-metre world record still stands. Bailey is also the only person to be inducted into Canada's Sports Hall of Fame twice. Since retirement from athletics in 2001, he has worked as a commentator for CBC, CTV and Eurosport. A lifelong entrepreneur and philanthropist, he now serves as a board advisor for several companies and is involved with and supports many charitable associations.